BORODINO

AND THE WAR OF 1812

by

Christopher Duffy

Charles Scribner's Sons

NEW YORK

Printed in Great Britain

Library of Congress Catalog Card Number 72-5758
SBN   684-13173-0   (cloth) Dec, 3, 1975

CONTENTS

ILLUSTRATIONS

Colour Plates
Between Pages 104 and 105

Black and White	Facing Page

7

MAPS AND DIAGRAMS

'At Borodino, as at Waterloo, lines were opposed to lines, man to man, and the appeal was made to each individual soldier's courage: the issue depended upon the exertion of power rather than the delicacy of manoeuvre or the caprices of fortune; the example of the chiefs, the charge, the storm, the repulse and the stand were the only tactics; the cross fire of cannon the only operation of strategy.' (Sir Robert Wilson *A Sketch of the Military and Political Power of Russia*, in the Year 1817, 3rd ed. London 1817, 27.)

INTRODUCTION

On 7 September, 1812, the armies of the French and Russian empires closed in deadly combat on the western approaches to Moscow. Altogether 258,000 men were engaged on a frontage of less than three miles in what the Russian commander, Kutuzov, called the 'most bloody battle of modern times'.[1] Other participants say that 'the ground trembled for a dozen miles around',[2] and that 'anyone who saw this battle has a fair idea of what hell must be like'.[3] In Napoleon's phrase this was truly 'a battle of giants'.

By the time the armies had done, they left the ground strewn with the bodies of 94,000 men and horses. Napoleon's force, although gravely weakened, pushed on to Moscow, while Kutuzov drew off his army in good order and made preparations for the counter-attack that was to drive the Westerners from the soul of Holy Russia.

Borodino was not one of those 'decisive battles' which present us with undisputed victors or vanquished at the end of the day's bloody work, but Napoleon failed in his aim of destroying the Russian army in a single, war-winning Armageddon of a combat. Thereafter every day he spent in Russia served to make the final ruin of his own army more complete. To that extent one of the Soviet historians is right to claim that 'the Battle of Borodino dealt the first powerful blow to Napoleon as the dictator of all Europe.'[4]

The Battle of Borodino and the campaign of 1812 have a very special place in the history of the Russians, for the resistance to the invaders was strengthened by the first upsurge of the modern Russian national consciousness, a power which has proved to be at once the servant and the master of subsequent governments. In 1941, Stalin had to authorize the reverence of certain military heroes and episodes of tsarist times, and the Soviet authorities regard an awareness of the military past as one of the most potent unifying forces at work in Russia to-day. At Borodino and in Moscow they have set up special museums to the glorification of Kutuzov and the Russian army of 1812 –

11

these attract crowds of Russians and are shown with pride to the foreign visitor. To understand what happened at Borodino is therefore to understand more than a little about Russia itself.

The rest of us have inherited a folk memory of that campaign which is compounded of snatches of Tchaikovsky's famous overture (best heard in the open air), the impression of some of the more striking episodes of Tolstoy's *War and Peace*, and the images of posturing horsemen, bleak landscapes and shattered cannon which are presented to us in illustrations and films. We in the West are not committed to conjuring up relevant justifications or parallels from the past, but we are all drawn to particular happenings on account of their inherent narrative value and human interest. That is why I have let the story of Borodino as far as possible 'tell itself' in the words of combatants on both sides who have described the battle.

My own interest in the Battle of Borodino began many years ago when I rescued an aura-ridden French carbine of 1812 which had found its way to a London junk-shop. Afterwards, at Sandhurst, I found myself in the Department of Military History and in the company of such experts in the Napoleonic period of military history as Brigadier Peter Young, Antony Brett-James, David Chandler and Richard Holmes. There cannot be many other institutions in the United Kingdom where the most solemn discussions of business are liable to be interrupted by speculations as to the length of Murat's plume or the nature of Kutuzov's off-duty activities. Thus primed, I visited Russia in 1970 for an historical congress and, like so many foreign travellers, was impressed by the expertise which the Russians have brought to the preservation and display of their battlefields and military relics.

The notion of writing the present book was conceived in the following year, when I was forced to collect my thoughts on the Battle of Borodino as a member of a team engaged in the filming of a television serial of *War and Peace*. For a short time the wildest dreams of a military historian came true – the heat, the smoke, the dust, the soldiers and the commission to design a new 'Raevsky Redoubt' in a lower Danubian desert. It was satisfying to see a column of 'French' soldiers throw themselves on the work and claw at the sides in a vain attempt to break in.

I am grateful to all the people who have helped me to accumulate these experiences, and particularly David Chandler, who has given me the benefit of his unrivalled knowledge of Napoleonic warfare, and Antony Brett-James for the kind permission to plunder his rich library of the military literature of the period.

David Chandler and Michaeljohn Harris have generously made photographs available for use in this book. I would also like to express my thanks to Boris Weltman who drew the maps.

Chapter 1

THE ROOTS OF THE WAR OF 1812

For centuries Europe had trembled whenever the rulers of France committed the material and human resources of the largest united population in the West to a major war. Their armies were tenacious and resourceful on the defensive, and they carried war into enemy lands with an *élan* which came to be recognised as typically French. Most of Europe had been forced to take up arms at the turn of the seventeenth and eighteenth centuries to contain the power of Louis XIV. The ambitions of his successors were more modest, and the prestige of the French army was for a time eclipsed by the shattering defeat which Frederick of Prussia inflicted on Marshal Soubise at Rossbach in 1757. However, French industries and arts continued to flourish, and over the next three decades a new generation of tacticians and military thinkers rebuilt the royal army on sound foundations.

In 1789 the pent-up energies of the French nation were released by the Revolution. At home the leadership of the movement was whisked away from the first aristocratic constitutionalists by a succession of demagogues and regicides, and finally came to rest in the shaky hands of the Directory, a committee of mediocrities who were all glad to accept the help of a gifted young artillery officer, Napoleon Bonaparte, in disciplining a shocked, divided but still feverishly excited population. Abroad, the Revolution devolved into a crusade against the states of monarchical Europe, and here too Napoleon made himself invaluable, campaigning with notable success against the Austrians in Italy in 1796-97 and again in 1800.

The Peace of Amiens brought an end to the first period of the Revolutionary wars in 1801, and Napoleon proceeded to consolidate his position as undisputed master of France. Already First Consul, he became Consul for Life in 1802, and crowned himself Emperor of the French two years later. He did what he could to mend the torn fabric of French society. He reached a modus vivendi with the Vatican, created a new code of laws and built up a centralized administration. In place of the old Bourbon monarchy he assiduously propagated a mystique of Imperial sovereignty, and surrounded himself with all the trappings of an aristocracy of his own creation: an ex-smuggler like Masséna could appear new-born as Marshal of France, Duke of Rivoli and Prince of Essling, though Napoleon (still a Corsican at heart) preferred to reserve the highest positions of trust for men who were related to him by blood or marriage.

Unfortunately for Europe, Napoleon managed to transmute and channel the militant drive of the old Revolutionary armies into a force which served his almost insatiable ambition for empire. He once explained that he 'in no way resembled those kings by divine right, who can consider their states as their inheritance. People like that may profit by tradition but for me it is an obstacle. Hated by its neighbours, and having to hold down various malcontents at home as well as to stare down so many enemies abroad, the French state stands in need of brilliant deeds and consequently of war. It must be the foremost of states or it must perish.'[1] The turn of phrase is decidedly Hitlerian.

In 1805, therefore, Napoleon embarked upon a new series of wars which were to last, with a few short respites, until his final downfall in 1815. The other Continental powers sought to hold him back by forming coalitions after the eighteenth century style, but there was little co-ordination or impetus apart from that afforded by the offer of English money, and the slow-moving monarchical armies proved no match for the aggressive forces of Napoleon. The Emperor routed a combined Austrian and Russian army at Austerlitz in Moravia in 1805, and knocked the Austrians out of the ring for the next four years. The Prussian main force did not survive long, being crushed at Jena in 1806, and Napoleon went on to settle accounts with the Russians. General Bennigsen fought the French to a near-draw at Eylau in February, 1807, but he was badly beaten at Friedland on 14 June, and Napoleon could begin to think of what terms he should accord to the King of Prussia and the young Russian Tsar, Alexander I.

The emperors of France and Russia met on apparently amicable terms on a decorated raft which was moored in the River Niemen at Tilsit. Alexander came in a state of not-unpleasurable tension. He was anxious to do well for his people, and it seemed to him that there was a real hope of obtaining a firm peace, if not much profit, from a man-to-man talk with Napoleon. For his part Napoleon behaved charmingly towards the impressionable Russian, who was seven years his junior. There were declarations of mutual regard and co-operation, with much hanging on of orders and decorations, and Napoleon conceded that he was perfectly willing to see the Russians make conquests at the expense of Sweden and Turkey. In return Alexander agreed to support Napoleon's economic blockade of Great Britain – the famous 'Continental System'. Altogether it seemed as if Russia had escaped as lightly as could have been expected after a major military defeat.

Napoleon was much harsher with the Prussians, who no longer had an effective army. He wasted no time in polite formalities, and tore away great chunks of the King's territories to help build up the Frankenstein's monster of satellite states which he was assembling beyond the already greatly-extended borders of old France: Prussian Poland went to the Grand Duchy of Warsaw, while Prussian Westphalia was incorporated in a new kingdom which was to be constituted under the rule of Napoleon's brother Jérôme.

The cowed and beaten monarchs might sign away freedoms and territory as if they were still living in the middle of the eighteenth century when national feelings were at a low ebb, but many of their subjects now felt that their nationhood and religion were endangered by the arrogance of the French. Within a couple of years of the meeting at Tilsit, therefore, Napoleon's armies began to encounter men who were fighting with at least as much enthusiasm as the French themselves had done at the height of their revolutionary fervour in 1793. The Spanish people took up arms in 1808, and the Austrians, transported by the general mood, declared war on the French in the following year. Napoleon came down the Danube to finish off the Austrians in person, but the whitecoats fought back unexpectedly hard and the Emperor suffered the first

17

severe check of his military career in the two-day action of Aspern-Essling (21–22 May, 1809), before he finally managed to break the resistance of the enemy at Wagram (5–6 July).

In the Peninsula the Spanish regular troops were defeated in detail by the French generals, but the *guerrilleros* prolonged the struggle until the British and Portuguese armies compelled Napoleon to send more and more forces to this distant and unprofitable part of the Continent. Meanwhile liberal-minded patriots were gaining influence among the Prussians and within the Napoleonic Empire proper the Continental System was causing widespread disruption and resentment.

All of this would have subjected the agreement between Napoleon and Alexander to great strain with the best will on both sides. As it was, in 1810 Napoleon threw away the chance of forging a dynastic link, when he spurned a sister of the Tsar and married instead the Archduchess Marie Louise of Austria. Hence there was no countervailing influence to those Russian ministers who warned of the danger of Napoleon establishing an independent state of Poland, or to the feelings of patriotism stirred up by some of the nobles, especially those who suffered from the end of the profitable timber trade with Great Britain.

By August, 1811, Alexander had shaken himself free from the agreements which had bound him to the French, and Napoleon had made up his mind to subdue Russia once more by armed force. He assembled 510,000 French and satellite troops for the attack and, on the night of 23/24 June, 1812, the advance guard crossed from the Grand Duchy of Warsaw over the River Niemen into Russia.

Chapter 2

THE WEAPONS AND TACTICS OF 1812

We can better understand the War of 1812 if we first examine the technical capabilities of the forces involved – the arms and the troops, and how they were managed in combat.

In the early nineteenth century, as at nearly every other time, the burden and decision of the battle rested chiefly on the infantry. The principal weapon of the infantry was a smooth-bore, muzzle-loading flintlock musket, of a design which had remained virtually unaltered since about 1700. In essence the musket consisted of a wooden-mounted iron tube some three feet long, with a bore of about three-quarters of an inch. At the breech end the barrel was closed, except for a narrow hole which was drilled through the side to communicate with a little metal trough called the 'priming pan', which formed part of the lock mechanism at the right-hand side of the breech. The priming pan was covered by the 'frizzen', a hinged flap which was knocked forward when it was struck by the flint which was held in the jaws of a little vice at the head of a pivoting hammer.

The usual sequence of loading was as follows. The musketeer put his hand into the cartridge pouch slung over his right hip and drew out a cartridge: this was a cylinder of cartridge paper which contained a measure of black powder and a leaden musket ball. He bit off the end of the cartridge, retained the ball in his mouth and (remembering not to swallow) cocked the hammer, shook a little powder from the opened cartridge into the priming pan and shut the frizzen. He emptied the rest of the powder down the barrel, spat the musket ball after it, screwed up the cartridge paper and poked it inside to serve as a wad. Lastly, the whole charge was driven to the bottom of the barrel by a long metal rod called the 'rammer'. The rammer was withdrawn and the musket was ready to fire.

When the trigger was squeezed the hammer swivelled violently forward and downwards, which scraped the flint against

19

the frizzen, knocking it forward and sending a shower of sparks into the priming pan. The powder in the pan ignited with a plume of smoke, and a moment later the main charge propelled the bullet from the barrel to the accompaniment of a dull boom.

The things that could go wrong with this complicated procedure were many and spectacular. Frequently the powder 'flashed in the pan' without communicating the flame to the charge inside the barrel. A musket which thus 'hung fire' was in a dangerous condition, for the charge could go off at any time. However, in the excitement of action musketeers often failed to notice that their weapon remained silent and continued to load one charge after another, with catastrophic results if the first charge took fire. Barrel explosions were, in any event, fairly common, especially in the smarter regiments, where the metal of the muskets was worn down by constant scraping and polishing. The ramrod or rammer was a particularly clumsy piece of equipment: in action the soldier frequently stuck it in the ground beside him, and it was all too easy for him to move off and forget it; he also, on occasion, neglected to remove it from the barrel after loading, and fired it away with the bullet.

Other malfunctions were accepted as routine. The flint in the hammer became worn and chipped after about twenty rounds, which forced the soldier to readjust the stone in the jaws of the vice or replace it altogether. A few rounds more and the inside of the barrel became so choked with carbon deposit that the charges were increasingly difficult to load, unless the musketeer stopped to scrape or wash the obstruction away.

At the best of times the performance of the musket was limited. There were no spiral grooves to impart a spin to the bullet and steady it on its course (as in the modern rifle), and in any case the ball was so loose-fitting that it progressed down the barrel in a series of shallow zig-zags, leaving the barrel in a prolongation of the last bound but one. The maximum effective range of such a weapon was reckoned to be about 250 yards, though even at a hundred yards it was hardly worth aiming at an individual (as opposed to a regiment). In any event only the coolest heads were capable of taking deliberate

20

aim in the heat of battle. Not surprisingly the tacticians calculated that 250 musket rounds were discharged in battle for
every man killed, a proportion which seems unduly high until
we recall that in modern wars the ratio is numbered in hundreds of thousands or even millions. When the musket ball did
strike home the effects were appalling. The soft bullet mush-
roomed out and imparted all its energy to the tissues, lifting a
man from his feet and inflicting a horrible funnel-shaped
wound.

Well-trained troops could deliver three rounds a minute on
the parade ground, but only a couple of rounds in battle conditions, a rate of fire which permitted enemy cavalry to come
within striking distance without suffering prohibitive casualties. In these circumstances the infantry had to put their trust
in the bayonet, a triangular-sectioned spike which was attached
by a metal sleeve to the muzzle of the musket. The short
infantry sword, or 'hanger', was a virtually useless survival
from past times. The sword was suspended over the left hip
from a belt which passed over the right shoulder, producing
the 'cross-belts' effect with the belt of the cartridge pouch.

We shall encounter three main categories of infantry. The
ordinary, unglamorous infantry of the line constituted the bulk
of every army. Then there were the various formations of
élite troops, entitled 'guards' or 'grenadiers', which were composed of men selected for their stature or bravery: these
valuable units were either held in reserve for special occasions,
or scattered among the other regiments so as to bolster up the
infantry of the line. Both the line battalions and the élite
troops usually moved and fought in shoulder-to-shoulder mass
formation. In contrast the third category, the light troops
(light infantry, chasseurs, voltigeurs, jaegers, etc.), were deployed ahead of the 'heavy' infantry in an extended order
which permitted them to take some advantage of the natural
cover of the ground. In the attack these screens of skirmishers
went forward to feel out the enemy and demoralize and pin
him down by their fire. The light infantry were just as useful
on the defensive, for they could absorb the first shock of the
enemy advance and put up an obstinate resistance from the
cover of forest or broken ground impassable to the formations
of line troops.

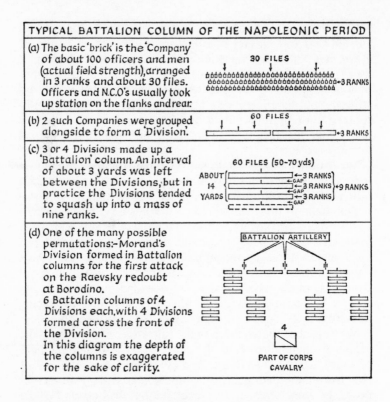

TYPICAL BATTALION COLUMN OF THE NAPOLEONIC PERIOD	
(a) The basic 'brick' is the 'Company' of about 100 officers and men (actual field strength), arranged in 3 ranks and about 30 files. Officers and N.C.O's usually took up station on the flanks and rear.	30 FILES · 3 RANKS
(b) 2 such Companies were grouped alongside to form a 'Division'.	60 FILES · 3 RANKS
(c) 3 or 4 Divisions made up a 'Battalion' column. An interval of about 3 yards was left between the Divisions, but in practice the Divisions tended to squash up into a mass of nine ranks.	60 FILES (50-70 yds) ABOUT 14 YARDS — 3 RANKS GAP — 3 RANKS GAP — 3 RANKS GAP · 9 RANKS
(d) One of the many possible permutations:- Morand's Division formed in Battalion columns for the first attack on the Raevsky redoubt at Borodino. 6 Battalion columns of 4 Divisions each, with 4 Divisions formed across the front of the Division. In this diagram the depth of the columns is exaggerated for the sake of clarity.	BATTALION ARTILLERY 4 PART OF CORPS CAVALRY

When a commander wished to produce the maximum weight of fire he would deploy the heavy infantry in lines of three ranks (rows) each, a formation which permitted all, or nearly all, the men to see the enemy and deliver a volley on command. The disadvantages of the line were felt when the men had to move forward, for the alignment was all too easily lost.

The solidity and mobility lacking in the three-rank line was supplied by the alternative formation, the column, the rather misleading name for a thick line up to eighteen or more ranks deep. Being much more compact than the line, the column could be directed at speed through a narrow passage or against a chosen sector of an enemy front. The column had been perfected by French tacticians in the 1780's as a means of moving troops over the battlefield until they came within a few hundred

22

yards of the enemy, upon which the component platoons would peel off to right and left to form a long three-rank line of battle of the kind already described. This 'deployment' from column to line was a tricky operation, and more and more frequently we find in the 1800's that undeployed columns were hurled into action in one piece, whether as an act of deliberate policy or simply because the troops came under fire before they could shake themselves out into line.

The fire-power of a column was negligible, but once the troops were in motion they were pushed forward by a moral and physical momentum which was sometimes capable of carrying them straight through an enemy line.

Although every nation cherished a myth of its superiority in hand-to-hand fighting, it was very rare indeed for intact formations to cross bayonets in the open field: when we hear of 'bayonet charges' we should imagine a line or column advancing at a steady pace with levelled bayonets against an enemy so badly shot-up as to be wavering or already in flight. A combat around fortifications or a battery was another matter, for the defenders were often strongly inclined to stay put (if only because they could not get out), and the attackers would be obliged to winkle them out by force.

Against an attack by cavalry the best defence for infantrymen was to form squares. The sides were three or more ranks deep, and experience showed that an intact square was virtually impregnable, for the fire of the massed musketry and the battalion guns, usually placed at the corners of the square, was lethal, while the upward-sloping bayonets presented the cavalry with an impenetrable hedge of steel. Unfortunately the square offered a magnificent target to the artillery, and if the enemy was cunning enough to bring his cannon up to canister range and open fire between the charges of the cavalry, then the square suffered very heavily indeed – as happened at Borodino to three Russian Lifeguard regiments. Under these circumstances a square might well be overrun, and the more experienced of the infantrymen then threw themselves on the ground where at least they had a chance of survival, for it was difficult for the cavalrymen to reach down so far with their swords, and horses hate to tread on any living object.

If 'shock action' by the infantry was something of a fantasy, it still retained all its primitive force among the cuirassiers, those lineal descendants of the mediaeval knights. Big armoured men on big horses, their job was to barge and hew their way through the main force of the enemy formations and ride down the broken regiments.

The rest of the cavalry went by a bewildering variety of titles (dragoons, mounted grenadiers, gensdarmes) mounted chasseurs, hussars and lancers) which signified differentiations in uniform and historical origin rather than any important specialization in their work. These medium and light cavalrymen took up position alongside the cuirassiers in the main line of battle, but in addition they carried out all the tasks in which mobility was at a premium – reconnaissance, pursuit, escort duties and harassing raids. Generally speaking the light cavalry (especially the hussars) were charged with the operations which were furthest away from the body of the army.

According to another rule of thumb, the lighter the category of cavalry the more pronounced the curve in the blade of its sabre. The straight sword of the cuirassier was ideally suited for pointing, which was a more effective way of using cold steel than slashing with the edge, but the most deadly and versatile of the cavalry weapons was the light, steel-tipped wooden lance, which was used by the regiments of uhlans on both sides in the Battle of Borodino. Not only could a good lancer unseat or spit an enemy cavalryman, he could also poke about to good effect in squares of infantry while remaining out of reach of the bayonet points.

In addition all cavalrymen were issued with a variety of fairly useless pistols or carbines. These had to be discharged at very short range to produce any effect, and the cavalry unit which slowed down to re-load or open fire ran a grave risk of being overturned by any force of enemy cavalry which came on with cold steel.

Historical paintings and films have created the cavalry charge's image of thundering hooves and flying manes, with hordes of yelling horsemen hurtling across the battlefield. In reality the cavalry charge was a short-winded affair, begun with some circumspection at a range of about three hundred yards. Gradually the speed built up through the trot to the canter and the gallop; only when about fifty yards from the enemy were the horses given their heads. By 1812 the continental cavalry (as opposed to the British) had perfected the art of rallying for a fresh attack after each charge, but at the end of a hard day's fighting in long grass the attack might be at little more than a walk. Strangely enough it greatly lessened the shock of an enemy attack if it was met by a counter-charge, since the opposing cavalrymen tended to bump past each other instead of engaging in a standing mêlée.

In the whole of military history there seem to be only three authenticated instances of infantry bold enough to charge cavalry with the bayonet – the Prussian regiment of Bernburg, which fell on the Austrian horse at Liegnitz in 1760, the Litovsk Lifeguards who attacked Murat's cavalry at Borodino (see p. 114, and the 5th Foot* at El Bodon in 1811.

For every man who was killed at Borodino by cold steel, there were scores who fell to the musket bullet and hundreds who were slaughtered by artillery. The guns, the great killers, were giant versions of the infantry musket. Their brass barrels weighed several hundredweight each and rested on stoutly-built wheeled carriages of wood. Powder (in bagged charges), wad and the missile were rammed down the barrel in much the same way as with the musket, though in infinitely greater quantity: the charge alone might weigh three or four pounds, and the explosion rocked the ground for hundreds of yards around. Ignition was achieved by applying a linstock or port-fire to the loose powder or to a small powder-filled tube which was introduced into the touch-hole at the breech. The aim was adjusted laterally by picking up the trail of the gun carriage and traversing the cannon bodily to right or left. To alter the elevation, the barrel pivoted up and down on the carriage, secured by a wedge inserted beneath the breech.

The conventional cannon came in two ranges of weights. The lighter guns like the four- and six-pounders (so called from the weight of solid shot they fired) were defined as battalion pieces and were used to lend close support to the infantry. The eight- or twelve-pounders, heavier and less mobile, were kept in reserve or assembled in batteries from where their fire-power could dominate whole sectors of the battlefield.

The solid, cast-iron roundshot was the principal missile of

* The Northumberland Fusiliers

25

the artillery. When fired at full elevation it travelled anything from 1,200 yards to a mile, depending on the calibre of the piece, and bounced along for several hundred yards more. A ball in full flight could plough through a score of men, and had considerable crushing effect even when rolling through the grass; recruits had to be restrained from trying to stop them with their feet.

For short-range work, below 400 yards, the artillerymen turned their cannon into monster shotguns by firing canister rounds; these were lightly-built cylinders of sheet metal which enclosed hundreds of musket balls or cast-iron shot about the size of walnuts. The cylinder disintegrated as it left the muzzle and the shot sprayed out over a wide arc.

Explosive shells had brittle cast-iron casings, and could only be fired from special artillery, like the Russian unicorns or the Western howitzers, which had 'chambered' barrels accommodating only a small powder charge. The flame of the discharge automatically ignited a slow-burning fuze plugged into the side of the shell. The fuze was adjusted (by cutting) to blow the bursting charge at the moment the shell struck the ground. Since black powder had a considerable incendiary effect these shells proved particularly effective against ammunition carts, though the lightness of the shell and the propelling charge told against accuracy and range. So far only the British had developed shrapnel proper, in the form of a canister shell which burst in the air over the heads of the enemy: when Continental gunners effected an air-burst it was only because they had cut their fuzes wrongly.

Provided he was given the time, a commander on the defensive could do a great deal to turn a battleground to his advantage. By clearing obstructions and making paths behind his front, he would be able to shuttle his reserves up and down the line with greater ease on the day of battle. Conversely he could hinder the enemy movements by demolishing bridges or forming barriers of felled trees called 'abattis'.

The batteries of heavy guns were often sited in earthworks which were so strong as to resemble miniature fortresses. The cannon were planted about eighteen feet apart (between muzzles) on platforms of planks, which prevented the wheels from sinking into the ground, and the barrels projected through

26

embrasures which were cut through a thick parapet of earth piled up in front of the guns. A broad, deep ditch was cut on the side of the battery which faced the enemy, so as to furnish the spoil for the parapet and also to offer an obstacle. Stakes were frequently used to afford additional defence: they might be planted upright in a palisade, or they could be stuck around the outer side of the parapet as 'storm poles'. In the jargon of the time 'redoubt' was the word for an enclosed battery with an all-round defence. An arrow-shaped battery which was open to the rear was termed a 'flèche' or 'redan'.

In most theatres of war the villages and farmhouses were built solidly enough to be converted into very formidable strongpoints, as witness the farms of Hougoumont and La Haye Sainte at Waterloo. In Russia, however, the timber villages were liable to become infernos, and a commander was well advised to dismantle them beforehand and use the wood for palisades or gun-platforms.

Compared with the dimensions of modern combat, the early nineteenth century battle was concentrated to an almost inconceivable degree, and the issue was usually decided by a single day's fighting in which all the available forces were committed to the fray or stood in immediate support. Ranges of weapons were short and the methods of transport were primitive, so an entire army could be packed row-upon-row into a space where a present-day battalion would feel unduly cramped, and the field at Borodino was restricted even by the standards of those times. Yet even the most hard-fought twentieth century campaigns would take weeks of time and miles of space before the butcher's bill exceeded the slaughter of a single day of battle in Napoleon's era. By comparison, in the Italian campaign of 1943 and 1944, from the landings at Salerno to the fall of Rome, the Allied Fifth Army lost hardly any more men than the French lost at Borodino in eleven hours and in a space of three and a half miles.

The means of controlling armies had progressed little, if at all, since the middle ages. Observation was still firmly earthbound (though Kutuzov would have dearly liked to have had a balloon at Borodino), and messages had to be carried to their destinations by mounted orderlies. Far more than in later times, an army commander was expected to see and supervise things for himself. His physical and mental states were therefore of supreme importance in deciding the outcome of a battle.

Chapter 3

NAPOLEON'S ARMY

The rival forces which met at Borodino were very evenly matched. Napoleon's army, hitherto almost invincible, was betraying slight but unmistakable signs of decay. The performance of the Russians had been unimpressive in the earlier Napoleonic wars, but the army which fought at Borodino was one of the best that they ever put into the field.

Up to now Napoleon had directed his armies in a way which explains why even his most bitter enemies could call him 'the God of War' (Clausewitz). It is still difficult to speak of such a monstrous phenomenon as Napoleon in anything but the tritest terms, but a saying which certainly applies is the one to the effect that 'genius is an infinite capacity for taking pains'. Quite simply, Napoleon in his prime worked harder and more effectively than any other general of his time. His grasp and retention of detail were extraordinary, and his army lived and moved entirely according to his dictates. At his fingertips he had a filing system which told him all he needed to know about every French and foreign unit, and he owned a superb collection of up-to-date maps over which he used to crawl when he was planning his campaigns. All his glittering suite, his aides, the thousands of officers and men of his headquarters, even his chief of staff, the jovial busybody Marshal Berthier, were little more than executive instruments of his will.

Napoleon was the deliberate creator of his own myth. Like Hitler, he regarded his adopted nation with detachment and not a little contempt, yet both men could mesmerize foreign statesmen and their own generals at will, and both managed to keep the loyalty of their armies to the very end. Napoleon used to ride up and down his lines of battle, greeting scarred veterans whom he recognized, or pretended to recognize, from past campaigns. Sometimes he halted in front of a battered regiment 'and there he would find out if any officers' places had fallen vacant, and ask in a loud voice the names of the men most

29

worthy to fill them. He called up the men who were pointed out to him and he proceeded to interrogate them: How many years of service did they have? What campaigns had they been through? What wounds had they suffered? Had they performed any brilliant deeds? He then promoted them officers and had them commissioned there and then in his presence ... all these little details were calculated to entrance the soldiers.'[1]

Over the years Napoleon had perfected a repertoire of effective strategic and tactical ploys. There was the wide envelopment which utilized the unrivalled marching power of the French armies and placed them in the rear of the disorganized enemy. Then there was the 'strategy of the central position', by which Napoleon struck at several enemy armies in succession, destroying them piecemeal before they could combine against him. In Russia, as we shall see, he planned to use features of both strategies to drive straight through the centre of the Russian armies.

On the battlefield he was adept at pulling the enemy off-balance by launching a feint attack against one flank or wing; sooner or later part of the enemy line became dangerously attenuated whereupon Napoleon would blast open a gap with massed canister fire from his reserve artillery, and send forward powerful columns of infantry and cavalry to penetrate the breach. Very occasionally, as at Rivoli on 14 January, 1797, he would eschew all manoeuvre and accept the risk of a purely frontal battle.

Before 1812 the French armies had almost invariably been lighter on their feet than their enemies, thanks largely to Napoleon's ruthless policy of dispensing with supply trains and tented camps, and letting his men seek food and shelter from the land. In 1805, while marching to join Napoleon at Austerlitz, Marshal Davout drove the head of a corps eighty-eight miles in just over forty-eight hours.

Davout was justly famous for his frugal and self-reliant habits. On the advance to Borodino the troops in his well-regulated I Corps carried haversacks holding 'the strict minimum of clothing, namely two shirts, two pairs of shoes with nails and spare soles, a pair of trousers, half-gaiters of cloth, a few items of cleaning kit, a bandage, some lint and sixty cartridges.

'The soldier had four biscuits, of sixteen ounces each, stuffed in the sides of the haversack. Down at the bottom there was a long and thin cloth sausage filled with ten pounds of flour. The haversack, complete with straps and the rolled-up overcoat which was attached to the top, weighed altogether thirty-three pounds, twelve ounces.

'In addition every soldier carried a cloth sack worn like a bandolier and holding two loaves of three pounds each. Thus, with his sword, his filled cartridge pouch, three flints, his screw-driver, his bandolier and his musket, the soldier was laden with fifty-eight pounds. He had bread and biscuit for four days, seven days' supply of flour, and sixty rounds of powder and ball.'[2] It remained to be seen how the army as a whole would fare on the road through Poland and Russia, where there were precious few provisions to be had, and where Napoleon was forced to rely on the old eighteenth century system of magazines and supply waggons.

In 1812, Napoleon was in his forty-fourth year but already a little way advanced along the path of physical and mental decline. At Austerlitz, almost seven years before, he had talked about one of the old Republican generals: 'Ordener is burnt out. We are granted only a limited time for making war; I give myself another six years, after which even I ought to come to a stop.'[3]

The scale of the theatre and the size of the armies in the Russian campaign would have stretched the capacities of any commander, let alone one like Napoleon who had to bear the responsibility of running an empire as well. Now, when most in need of all his faculties, he succumbed to a bladder complaint (cystitis) which was liable to strike him down whenever he was overstressed by exercise or strong emotion. Megalomania and delusion began to take the place of rational calculation and, like some ageing *capo* of a Mafia clan, he lived in mistrust of all but the members of his immediate family. His plan for the initial offensive in 1812 collapsed partly because he chose to entrust his incapable and wilful brother Jérôme with an important command on the right wing.

For several decades the French had been evolving a military machine at once more complex and more responsive than the simple structure of regiment and army, which was all that had

31

been known in the middle of the eighteenth century. By 1812 the largest single subdivision was the *corps d'armée,* a miniature army which had a nominal strength of anything between 20,000 and 75,000 men, composed of a varying number of infantry divisions together with an attached division or brigade of light cavalry and a powerful complement of heavy artillery. Napoleon took seven such corps into Russia. The bulk of the cavalry was concentrated in the four reserve cavalry corps – bodies of 10,000 or more horsemen each, a most imposing sight on the battlefield.

We descend by way of divisions and brigades of varying strength to the infantry regiment of 1812, which fought at Borodino with two battalions, each comprising six companies. The size of the company stood at a nominal 140 men and the regiment as a whole at about 1,680, though these numbers were hardly ever attained in reality. Among its six companies the battalion owned one company of tall, fierce grenadiers, and another of nimble light-infantrymen called *voltigeurs.*

In theory French infantry tactics were based on the Drill Book of 1791, which enjoined the use of the column for most movements on the battlefield, but stressed the advantages of deployment into line in order to attain the maximum firepower in combat. From at least 1809, however, we find that the French usually abandoned the niceties of the parade ground and waded into the fight in undeployed columns (see p. 22), with the *voltigeurs* working ahead as a sharpshooter screen.

Of all the possible permutations of battle formation, perhaps the most frequently used was the battalion column, or column of divisions, in which the battalion advanced three companies deep on a two company front. Each of the three lines was three ranks deep, and the whole mass measured seventy yards long by fifteen deep. A space of at least 150 yards was left between each of the battalion columns so as to permit the light infantry to fall back and allow room for deploying into line.

As if the firepower of the French was not sufficiently weakened by such columnar tactics, the infantrymen were armed with the Model 1777 Charleville musket, a not particularly robust weapon of light calibre and liable to bad fouling from the coarse French powder. Napoleon suffered from a

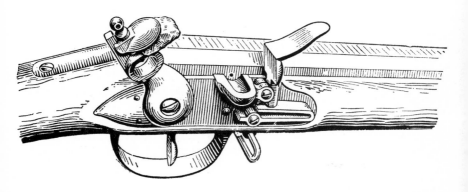

1 Musket Lock. The hammer has been drawn back to full cock. On the right the hinged frizzen is in the forward position, uncovering the priming pan.

2 Twelve-pounder Russian cannon, (system of 1805).
The elevating wedge is driven by a screw.

3 Twelve-pounder Russian Unicorn Howitzer, (system of 1805).

4 Prince Eugène de Beauharnais, Napoleon's step-son. Commander of IV Corps and the left wing of the French army at Borodino.

blind spot on the subject of minor tactics, but the inadequacy of the French musketry was so glaring that he had to attach four four-pounder guns to each infantry regiment.

Within the *Grande Armée* the French cavalry proper consisted of the regiments of heavy cuirassiers and carabiniers (nominal strength 1,040 men, with four squadrons of two troops each), the dragoons (1,200 men, five squadrons), the *gensdarmes d'élite*, and the three types of light cavalry – the lancers, the hussars, and the numerous and colourful *chasseurs à cheval* (1,200–1,800 each). The combat formations were made up of lines of two ranks each.

The Napoleonic artillery was based upon the range of guns which had been introduced by Jean Baptiste de Gribeauval in 1774. The heavy pieces, the twelve- and eight-pounder cannon, were usually held in corps or divisional reserve, ready to be brought forward when one of the senior commanders called for massive firepower. The numerous and mobile four-pounders were distributed among the army to provide close support to the infantry or formed into batteries of horse artillery to follow the movements of the cavalry. The six-inch howitzer, a notoriously inaccurate piece, was employed at all levels of the army. The artillery as a whole was usually divided into eight-piece batteries of six cannon and two howitzers.

Inside the *Grande Armée* of 1812 Napoleon had about 250,000 national French troops. They were no longer quite the equal of the men of the campaigns of 1805 or 1806. The army was recruited by a yearly levy of conscripts between eighteen and thirty, but already Napoleon was beginning to eat into his capital of manpower and was anticipating the call-up of younger persons. If affairs had not yet reached the desperate straits of 1813, when the ranks were filled with pathetic fifteen- or sixteen-year-old *Marie Louises,* the veterans were already acquiring something of a scarcity value: 'You could make them out by the martial cast of their features and the way they talked. War was the only thing they remembered and it was all they could look forward to. They had no other topic of conversation.'[4]

These precious reserves of seasoned troops were not deployed in the best way. Many of the finest men were creamed off into the Imperial Guard, which entered the

Russian campaign about 46,000 strong. The Guard was never far away from the person of Napoleon, and provided him with a small army of battle-hardened and utterly devoted troops. Unfortunately the Guard shared vices which have been common to many élite formations in history: it owned a prior claim on manpower and equipment, thus starving the less glamorous units, and in the course of time it became too precious to be committed to battle. Indeed it seems that in his last years Napoleon did not know what to do with it: at Waterloo he threw in the Guard too late, while at Borodino he shrank from employing it at all.

Within the line regiments themselves the best private soldiers were promoted or were shunted into the grenadiers or *voltigeurs,* all of which told upon the quality of the rank and file of the centre companies.

In 1812 Napoleon had a high proportion of soldiers from other continental countries. To the north and south of the *Grande Armée* there marched powerful units of Prussians and Austrians, covering the strategic flanks, and at Borodino Napoleon entrusted entire sections of his front to foreign units. Following the line of battle from the right to left we find the Polish V Corps of Poniatowski, the Saxons and Poles in Latour-Maubourg's cavalry corps, the four regiments of the Legion of the Vistula, which were attached to the Guard, the Royal Württemburg infantry in Ney's III Corps with the Westphalians in Junot's corps behind, and the Italians and Bavarians who made up the greater part of Eugène's IV Corps on the right; there were also three regiments of Croats and Dalmatians, and such assorted units of shivering southerners as the two Spanish regiments, the two Portuguese, and the Mameluke cavalry from Egypt.

Even among the nominally French divisions perhaps only about two-thirds of the men hailed from old France. The metropolitan borders by now embraced Belgium, Holland, the left bank of the Rhine, part of Hanover, Geneva, Savoy, Avignon, Nice, Piedmont, Genoa, Parma and Tuscany.

For all the problems created by this diversity of equipment, tactics and tongues, these foreigners served Napoleon very well. The Poles fought with positive enthusiasm, since they identified Napoleon's cause with their own national quarrel

34

with the Russians. The Germans took a professional attitude to the war, and took a pride in disposing of the enemies of their paymaster in the shortest possible order. All nationalities could respond to the leadership of generals like Montbrun, who was popular among the Prussians, or Latour-Maubourg who entranced the moustachioed Saxons because 'he rode amazingly well, and had his horse meticulously cared for by a German groom called König'.[5] The Polish and German cavalry did invaluable service at Borodino, for the Frenchman was not really an *homme de cheval,* as Napoleon once admitted, and the French had lost many of their badly cared-for horses on the sandy roads through Poland and Russia.

Chapter 4

THE RUSSIAN ARMY

To the foreigner there are features of that vast organization, the tsarist army, which must always remain something of a mystery. Why, for instance, with some of the best potential military material in the world, did the commanders fail to sweep every opponent off the board? Or why did Russian soldiers nearly always fight with such perseverance and devotion when the armies were little better than armies of slaves?

The performance of the Russians in 1812 becomes a little more comprehensible when we appreciate some of the influences to which the army and the nation had been subjected over the last few decades.

The old Russia, half-mediaeval and half-oriental, had been shattered by Peter the Great (1672-1725), who began the formidable task of westernizing Russian life and institutions. He broke the power of the boyars (nobles), and created a new meritocracy to help him with the running of affairs. In military matters, as in so much else, Peter and his successors were impressed by the way things were managed in Prussia, the most tightly-run of all the German states. As a result, military development under the tsars can be seen as a kind of dialogue between two conflicting influences: on the one hand the mind-crushing, goose-stepping discipline of the Potsdam drill square, and on the other a brand of inspirational leadership capable of summoning up reserves of elemental force from the mass of the Russian nation.

Our period begins at a time when admiration for things German was tending to an extreme. In 1776, during the reign of Catherine the Great, her son the snub-nosed, dapper and diminutive Grand Duke Paul visited the Potsdam of Frederick the Great, and was entranced by the turn-out of the Prussian troops. On his return to Russia Paul converted a marshy estate at Gatchina into a miniature kingdom which was run on Prussian lines, complete with a ridiculously over-drilled army.

Paul became tsar in 1796, and immediately set about turning the Russian army into a replica of Frederick's army as it had been after the Seven Years War. He re-clad the troops in all the pomaded grandeur of the middle decades of the eighteenth century, and by his military code of November, 1796, he stressed the importance of rigidly linear tactics and the niceties of drill. Among other things he reduced the marching pace to a waddle of seventy-five steps a minute.

Alongside the new Russia of the westernising tsars there survived something of an older Russia, represented by the native aristocracy, with its resentment of foreign experts and favourites, and by a genuine nationalist feeling in the nation as a whole. Towards the end of the eighteenth century the Russian army found the kind of leadership it needed in Generalissimo Alexander Suvorov (1730-1800). Suvorov trained his armies on realistic lines; he was 'a leader quite out of and above the ordinary rules of military criticism,'[1] who appreciated that 'a man is not purely and simply a machine'[2] and strove against everything that was represented by the spirit of Gatchina. He dismissed the code of 1796 as 'a rat-eaten parchment found in a corner of an old castle,' and rejected the Prussian-style linear fire tactics in favour of the attack in mass formations with the bayonet.

Paul was assassinated by a conspiracy of nobles in 1801, and his gentle, upright and well-mannered son came to the throne as Tsar Alexander I. Few rulers of Russia have ever embarked on their task with such a wealth of good intentions as did Alexander, and hardly any have proved to be quite as incapable of following through their policies to the end. There was something unfinished about the man and almost everything he did: he was a voracious reader, but rarely reached the last page of a book; he possessed just enough military knowledge to disrupt the work of his generals, while lacking the confidence and ability to take command himself; above all he was too liable to be swathed by whatever strongly-phrased argument happened to be most recently presented to him.

We must give the new Tsar credit for having had the courage

to break with most of his father's policies, but in military affairs he remained for too long under the sway of the frightful Alexei Arakcheev, whom he made Inspector General of Artillery and, in 1808, Minister of War. While Arakcheev did good work for the artillery, the general effect of his administration was deplorable, prolonging the tyranny of Gatchina into the nineteenth century. Fortunately Arakcheev resigned in 1810, in protest against another minister's attempt to define the power of the Tsar in constitutional terms, and he was supplanted by Barclay de Tolly, a man who influenced the army profoundly for the good.

Mikhail Bogdanovich Barclay de Tolly (1761-1818) was born to a family of Scots origin, long settled among the Baltic Germans of Livonia. Totally without money or military connections, he soldiered for fourteen years as an NCO in a dragoon regiment until his unusual talents were noticed by Prince Repnin, who gave him a commission and made him his adjutant. Barclay became a major-general in the campaign of 1806-07, and as a lieutenant-general he commanded one of the three divisions which made the spectacular advance over the ice of the Gulf of Bothnia in the Russo-Swedish War of 1808-09.

Barclay's life and character fitted him admirably for the work of re-shaping the Russian army in time to meet the exigencies of the confrontation with France. One of his staff officers recalls that he was 'a straightforward, serious but friendly kind of person. He was not perhaps very intelligent, though he had a profound knowledge of mankind and he was an outstanding administrator.'[3] In wartime he proved to be 'a splendid fighting general' if not 'a leading strategist'.[4] By the time Barclay assumed office in 1810 he moved somewhat stiffly, thanks to his old wounds, though even now this pastor's son had about him something of the air of a professional man, a kindly headmaster perhaps, rather than one of the most experienced and battle-tested of the Russian generals.

The raw material upon which Barclay worked was a mass of more than a million serf-like soldiers, drawn almost entirely from the peasants who made up more than ninety-five per cent of Russia's population of forty-four million. The young men as a whole were hard and fit; indeed they sought relief from

38

the toil in the fields by staging rough rural sports such as the mass fist-fights in which entire villages used to take part. The local magistrates could therefore be highly selective in the choice of recruits, and they did not hesitate to reject men for such minor defects as bad teeth.

These countrymen made a magnificent infantry, 'composed of athletic men between the ages of eighteen and forty, endowed with great bodily strength, but generally of short stature, with martial countenance and complexion; inured to extremes of weather and hardship, to the worst and scantiest food, to marches for days and nights, of four hours repose and six hours progress; accustomed to hard work and to carrying heavy loads; ferocious, but disciplined; obstinately brave, and susceptible of enthusiastic excitements; devoted to their sovereign, their chief, and their country. Religious, without being weakened by superstition; patient, docile and obedient; possessing all the energetic characteristics of a barbaric people, with the advantages engrafted by civilization.'[5] The Russians were formidable in the attack, if not particularly dashing. On the defensive they displayed a bovine endurance, clinging together in dense masses in which the living were jammed together with the dying and the dead. As Frederick the Great found in the Seven Years War, and the British were to discover in the Crimea, it was not enough simply to kill Russians – you had to knock them down as well.

The troops were conscripted by sporadic levies on the 'souls' which were entered on the tax rolls. It is some indication of the size of the population that a levy of one 'soul' out of five hundred could produce 32,000 recruits. In some years no conscription took place at all, whereas in 1812 alone the government imposed three levies, each of up to five men on every hundred 'souls'.

The term of service was twenty-five years, and the families of the conscripts knew that short of a miracle they had no hope of seeing their men again. The relatives were grief-stricken when the magistrates pronounced the doom, but as soon as the recruit's head had been shaved, as the first sign of military service, the family gave itself up to merrymaking and sent him on his way with their congratulations. The children of soldiers had no chance of escaping from military

39

servitude. These wretched 'cantonists' were consigned to special schools, nicknamed 'stick academies', where they were beaten into shape for a military career.

The adult recruits were sent to one of the twenty-six or so recruit-training depôts which had been set up a few years before the war – the infantry depôts in 1808 and the cavalry depôts in 1809. Altogether between fifty and sixty thousand men were being processed in these establishments at any time. The active forces possessed a further reserve in the shape of the Supply Army, which was composed of the second battalions of the infantry regiments and one out of every six squadrons of cavalry, which remained on the home grounds of the regiments and acted as sources of replacements for the first and third battalions and the active squadrons. Shortly before the War of 1812 the Supply Army was reorganized as an active support force of eight divisions of infantry (106,000 men) and three divisions of cavalry (12,412). The grenadier companies of the second battalions remained permanently with the field armies, and were formed into the combined grenadier battalions (two per division) which fought at Borodino.

Barclay organized the Russian infantry into corps on the French model. Each corps was composed of two divisions of infantry, with one or more companies of artillery and a regiment or brigade of cavalry. In turn each division was made up of three brigades – two brigades of line infantry and one of jaegers (light infantry). The brigade was made up of two regiments of three battalions each (including the second battalion with the Supply Army). In 1812 the actual strength of a battalion stood at about eight hundred men, who were divided among three companies of musketeers and one of grenadiers.

The grenadier company was divided into two platoons. The first platoon was made up of grenadiers proper and stood on the right of the battalion. The second was the jaeger platoon and stood on the left – an obvious crib from the French system of centre companies, grenadiers and *voltigeurs.*

Until Barclay reformed the organization of the battalion in 1810, the grenadiers and the jaegers had been selected by height (the taller men to the grenadiers, the smaller to the jaegers), and the jaegers had formed a third rank along the rear of the battalion, which was just about the worst possible position for their work. Barclay was determined that the grenadiers and jaegers should win their places by merit alone: 'The slightest fault will deprive the jaeger and the grenadier of his distinction, and by "fault" I mean not only carelessness in drill and similar mistakes, but any offence which is inconsistent with the good conduct and honour of a crack soldier.'[6]

When he assumed office Barclay was appalled by the way the adherents of the Gatchina school were maltreating the men. He pointed out that 'the Russian soldier possesses all the higher military virtues. He is brave, keen, devoted and reliable. Consequently we have no need to resort to cruelty in order to find means of training him and keeping him in order.'[7] Before Barclay took a hand the officers and NCOs used to subject the soldiers to barbaric punishments for trivial offences, and ground the spirit out of them by long and arduous sessions on the drill square; whole battalions were fading away from an unrelieved diet of bread, because the authorities were unwilling to allow the men the luxury of meat. In June, 1810, Barclay began the task of remedying these abuses. The shade of Suvorov must have looked on with approval.

The same brisk and intelligent spirit informed the new tactics. Arakcheev himself had introduced a 'quick' step of 110 paces to the minute to supplement the slow march, though on the parade ground both kinds were still carried out as a stiff-legged goose-step. Otherwise the emphasis was taken off drill and more time was devoted to practical training. Barclay wrote to the generals on 6 September, 1810, that 'the main occupation of a soldier's training should be shooting at a target. The men can become good marksmen only when their officers avoid all compulsion and have a fundamental understanding of the mentality of the soldier.'[8] He went into more detail in 1811 in the *Instructions for Target Practice.* He ordered a considerable quantity of powder to be set aside for training, and described how a target two yards high and just over two feet wide should be painted with horizontal stripes so as to accustom the men to elevating or depressing the musket barrel according to the range. In the *Code of Infantry Service,* also published in 1811, Barclay stressed that in

41

musketry instruction and every other kind of training the officers must 'refrain from dealing out punishment, and take care to explain the rules with patience, showing what ought to be done and how it ought to be done. When you are teaching you should reserve chastisement only for occasions of carelessness, though even here you must proceed with moderation and prudence'.[9]

It was a pity that the Russians were armed so badly that they could not take full advantage of their excellent training. The small arms factories at Sestrovetsk and Tula turned out between 150,000 and 170,000 weapons a year – clumsy pieces which were never reduced to a uniform system. In 1812 the Russians went to war with twenty-eight different calibres of infantry muskets, and eleven kinds of short rifles which were issued on the basis of sixteen to every squadron of cuirassiers and dragoons, and twelve to the NCOs and best shots of each jaeger company. Sixty thousand fine English muskets were given to the most deserving soldiers as rewards, which only added to the diversity.

In any case the Russians were still under the spell of the Suvorovian doctrine which held that the bayonet was the true Russian weapon, and that the push with the bayonet was far more decisive than musketry. The *Precepts for Infantry Officers on the Day of Battle*, which came to the Second West Army in June, 1812, stated that in the bayonet charge the true place of the officer was at the head of the men, and that this gallant individual 'could be sure that his subordinates, heartened by such an example, will never permit him to attack the enemy line alone'.[10] The obsession with deep formations reached its extreme in 1812, when virtually all the line infantry at Borodino was arranged in battalion columns in the French style.

Barclay's administrative and tactical system was applied throughout the infantry, and affected not just the line infantry but the grenadier regiments, the infantry regiments of the Imperial Guard and the jaeger regiments. The regiments of grenadiers are best described as a kind of super infantry, composed of men selected for their size and strength and distinguished by tall brass-fronted mitre hats. The very best recruits were assigned to the infantry of the Imperial Guard,

42

which was composed of four regiments of heavy infantry, and two of jaegers recruited principally in Siberia and Finland. Sir Robert Wilson observed of the Guard that 'there cannot be a nobler corps, or one of more warlike description, and the simplicity of the dress gives to the man the full character of his figure and mien'.[11] Like the grenadiers the guardsmen were chosen above all for their imposing appearance, and at the Tilsit conference of 1807 they made a much better impression than the little men of the French Imperial Guard, who were selected by merit alone and seemed to be crushed by their immense bearskin headgear.

The jaeger regiments made up nearly one-third of the total of the infantry (fifty regiments out of about 160). They were prized for their high morale, though they received little specific training as light infantry, and were equipped and armed in the same way as the other foot soldiers.

These permanent regimental grenadiers and jaegers should not be confused with the grenadiers and jaegers of the élite company of the line battalion.

At the beginning of operations in 1812 the Russian regular cavalry was composed of five regiments of heavy Lifeguard Cavalry, eight cuirassier regiments, thirty-six dragoon regiments, eleven regiments of hussars, three of uhlans (lancers) and some small units of Lifeguard Cossacks.

The largest single organization of Russian cavalry was the corps of three or four thousand riders, a formation which was dwarfed by the mighty combined cavalry corps which the French put into the field at Borodino. The Russian cavalry corps was composed of two divisions of three brigades each (two brigades in the case of the cuirassiers).

There were ten divisions in all. The two cuirassier divisions formed exclusive clubs of their own, but the other divisions were well-balanced forces which were made up most commonly of two brigades of dragoons and one of hussars with a lancer regiment sometimes thrown in. Two or sometimes three regiments made up the brigade. The regiment, of about 750 men, broke down into six squadrons (one of which was detached on depôt duty), and twelve half-squadrons of two platoons each.

The Russian hussars sported much the same gorgeous and

43

highly impracticable uniforms as their counterparts in other armies. The cuirassiers and dragoons wore metal-fronted, comb-tipped helmets in the Grecian style. The white-uniformed cuirassiers wore additional armour in the form of a heavy iron breastplate, lacquered in black, though in a spirit of misplaced heroism they scorned any cover for their backs. The dragoons had no protection save their padded green jackets.

The Russian cavalry put almost all its trust in cold steel – the straight broadsword of the cuirassiers and dragoons, the curved sabres of the hussars, and the lance of the uhlans and cossacks. In 1812, indeed, the standard carbines were withdrawn from all cavalry regiments, leaving sixteen men in each squadron with specialized firearms for their duty as flankers: the skirmishers of the heavy cavalry retained diminutive rifled carbines which were little more than stocked pistols, while the flankers of the hussars scattered small shot in every direction from an alarmingly unselective blunderbuss, the muzzle of which was in the shape of a flattened bell.

In 1812 a *Preliminary Decree Concerning the Order of the Cavalry Service* at last replaced the regulations which dated from Tsar Paul's time. The attack on the enemy could be carried out either in deployed order of two ranks, with the second immediately behind the first, or by the column of platoons which was described as 'the best formation for every kind of movement'. The charge gathered momentum gradually: it began with a fifty-pace walk, changed to a trot for one hundred paces, and broke into a gallop for eighty before giving way to a furious *carrière* in which the horses were given their head for eighty more. On either side of the main force the half-squadrons of sixteen men each swept forward in open order to guard the flanks.

The Russian cavalry was mounted on tough, fast, if not very beautiful, horses from the Don and the Volga. As for the officers, Wilson noted that they attended to their duties 'with great zeal and diligence'.[12] If the Russians had learnt to combine their cavalry in larger shock-formations on the battlefield it might have become the most formidable horse in Europe.

The Russian irregular cavalrymen, the cossacks, were the most exotic element in the entire army. They were the descendants of outlaws and refugees who had settled on the lower reaches of the great rivers of southern Russia under the command of their atamans, or chiefs. They constituted a permanent reserve of more than 100,000 men. Armed with lance, sword and pistol, they could ride for day after day at a steady five miles per hour, keeping up their spirits by the ingenious improvisations of their solo singers and the impact of their choruses – 'thundering peals of musical power and barbaric sublimity'.[13]

We do not see the cossacks at their best at Borodino. They were excellent at outpost work and reconnaissance; they could mount excellent ambushes and they were merciless in hunting down stragglers. In open combat, however, they did not prove particularly dangerous enemies. General Dumonceau, in his *Memoirs*, recalled that they made some noisy charges 'though if you keep up a bold front and are not intimidated by their deafening cries they will not press home the attack, but stop dead or fall back in order to prepare a new charge. The moment the artillery opens up they make themselves scarce. Threaten them with a pistol or any kind of firearm and they will keep out of your way. They never hold their ground or risk a personal combat unless they have odds in their favour of several to one.'[14]

Russian commanders were accustomed to fight with an extremely powerful artillery at their disposal, if only to make up for the comparative lack of manoeuverability of their infantry. The Russian artillery had fallen somewhat behind the times by the beginning of the century, and the army came to Austerlitz in 1805 with guns that were heavy, powder that was dirty and artillerymen who did not understand their job. Prince Orlov loudly remarked that it was entirely a matter of luck whether Russian gunners hit their target or not.

It was Alexei Arakcheev who was largely responsible for putting things right. The System of 1805 introduced a new range of twelve- and six-pounder cannon and twenty-, ten- and three-pounder 'unicorns'. These unicorns were long-barrelled howitzers of a type first designed by Danilov and Martinov in 1757, and they threw explosive shells with greater velocity and accuracy than the six-inch howitzer of the French. The three-pounder unicorn went out of use before the War of 1812, but the heavier models remained in service until the

Crimean War, after which many specimens found their way to Great Britain as prizes, where they may be recognized by the characteristic constriction at the exterior of the breech.

The elevating wedges of Arakcheev's guns were operated by screws, which gave greater accuracy, and the carriages as a whole were strong and light and equipped with admirable harness and tackle. The woodwork was painted apple green, and the brass barrels were rubbed until they shone like candlesticks. The Karbanov system of gun sights was fixed to the barrels in 1811. The lighter pieces were drawn by four of the strong but diminutive Russian draught-horses, eight or ten of which could pull a twelve-pounder into one side of a mountainous snowdrift and out the other.

The foundries at Bryansk, Ekaterinburg, Kamensk, Aleksandrovsk and other places were capable of casting eight hundred pieces a year for the armed forces, and great quantities of shot and shell were produced by the factories which had been established by Peter the Great in the Urals. As Wilson observed: 'No other army moves with so many guns, and in no other army is it (the artillery) in a better state of equipment.'[15]

In 1811 Barclay reorganized the artillery into twenty-seven field brigades, ten reserve brigades and four depôt brigades. The field brigade was usually on an establishment of two companies of light artillery and one of heavy, each company being composed of up to twelve pieces. The sixty-four guns of the Guard Artillery were on a separate roster of six companies.

Immediately before the outbreak of hostilities in 1812 Major-General Kutaisov published his *General Rules for the Artillery in Field Actions*. The job of the artillery on the attack, he said, was to knock out the opposing guns, but in a defensive battle it was better to concentrate one's fire against the infantry and cavalry. At a range of a thousand paces it was worth chancing a shot only to check the range or to interfere with enemy movements; at six hundred paces artillery fire could cause considerable disruption and delay, but only became really murderous when the enemy closed to 450 paces or less, in which case the gunners should fire as fast as possible.

Kutaisov recommended that massed batteries should be assembled to punch a hole in the enemy line or to hinder the enemy from breaking through at a particular point – another example of the influence of Napoleonic methods on the Russians of 1812. At the beginning of the battle, however, Kutaisov believed that it was a good idea to 'conceal the number of your guns, and then increase the quantity in action as the combat goes on.'[16] It so happened that at Borodino Kutaisov was killed before he could make use of the artillery reserves, with the result that many of the Russian guns never saw action at all.

In the Russian artillery the quality of the gunners and NCOs was generally high, though a gunner officer commanded little prestige in the army – the prototype of Tolstoy's Captain Tushin, who was blamed for having kept up the fight too long at Schöngraben in 1805. On the day of battle the overall command of the artillery all too often fell to some ill-qualified officer who happened to have caught the eye of the generalissimo.

The Russians had a long tradition of field engineering, and in 1797 Paul put affairs on a sound basis by setting up a corps of pioneers. By 1812 the pioneers made up two regiments with a total complement of 2,270 men, a tiny force which was to exercise an influence out of all proportion to its size on the field of Borodino.

The officer corps in general was a microcosm of the Russian upper classes, with its hard-working provincial 'Tushins', its brave, idle aristocrats, and its sprinkling of foreign careerists and adventurers. The paths of promotion were manifold. According to the old Russian custom, the potential officer was supposed to begin his career among the rank and file and gradually work his way upwards. A few men, like Barclay, went through the mill; many more learnt little but bad 'old soldier' habits and spent the rest of their working lives as ignorant, underpaid and totally obscure infantry officers.

Well-connected youths usually found easier roads. A young gentleman could enter the Page Corps, the Noble Land Cadet Corps, or one of the other cadet houses, and pursue a general and military education while being promoted through the ranks in *absentia*. A commission in the Guards or cuirassiers would be ready for him when he left his academy at about the age of twenty. If a young man was bent on a career in the line infantry, he could still avoid contact with the socially inferior junior infantry officers by spending a few years in one of the smarter regiments and then transferring to a less spectacular unit with a high rank.

Thanks to his German blood, the staff officer Friedrich von Schubert could look upon the system with the detachment of an outsider. He says that 'the Guards officers were the focal point of the balls and every other kind of society. They were notable for their education and good manners, if not for their morals, and the general effect was probably enhanced by the presence of the large number of émigres of the leading families of France who were serving there.'[17] Though the rigid social stratifications of the eighteenth century were already breaking up, 'during the first half of the reign of Tsar Alexander it was still rare to encounter an officer in the society of a merchant'.[18]

Once admitted to the charmed circle the young officer was welcomed to the gambling table and the quarters where his colonel held open house. The English officer Sir Robert Wilson testified that the Russian senior officers were 'liberal gentlemen, of kind dispositions, affable manners, and honourable conduct, with high independent feelings'[19] – the sort of statement which is usually delivered in a single breath and terminated by a hiccup.

The Russian officer was capable of great physical exertion when the demands of duty left him with no alternative. Otherwise he was in the habit of taking long siestas after food, and he avoided walking whenever possible. Alexander was astonished to find Wilson on foot in the streets of St Petersburg, and told him that he wished his own officers would take to the same exercise.

The foreign-born officers constituted a small but significant element during the War of 1812. The Tsars made a point of admitting likely officers of every nation and religion to the Russian service, and they allowed them a year in the country to learn the language before taking up staff or regimental duties. Three hundred or so Prussians – Phull, Wolzogen, Clausewitz and the like – came to Russia after the recent misfortunes of their native Prussia, and they quickly aroused

48

5 Joachim Murat, in full panoply with Vesuvius erupting in the background; King of Naples and overall Commander of Napoleon's cavalry in the 1812 Campaign.

6 Napoleon displays the portrait of the King of Rome to his
  admiring Imperial Guard.

7 Napoleon at Borodino. He is showing an evident lack of interest in the proceedings.

much resentment by their sinister and secretive ways and by the respect they seemed to command from the Tsar and some of his generals.

The foreigners were struck by a lack of professionalism in the higher échelons of the Russian army. Before the war the posts of Quartermaster-General and General-Adjutant were filled by Prince Volkonsky, who had the ambition, but scarcely the talent, to set himself up as the Tsar's Berthier. Alexander must have been aware that Volkonsky did little but fuss around collecting maps, yet the prince had once been his adjutant in the Guards and he found him a pleasant and undemanding companion.

Volkonsky could think of nothing better to do with the officers of his General Staff in St Petersburg but to set them to purely clerical tasks, so a staff officer who wanted some real work was 'constantly on the lookout for an opportunity to get himself posted to an office or job with a senior general in the provinces. His motivation was all the stronger since his pay was exceedingly small, while the luxury in St Petersburg was so great that the cost of living made it impossible for him to maintain a fitting style of life, without some addition to his salary.'[20]

Barclay's aide, von Schubert, writes that when his chief came to office in 1810 he saw 'that our army lacked any code which defined the duties and rights of every commander, or the make-up and sphere of activity of each department and office. These regulations were all the more necessary in view of the sort of war which was looming ahead.'[21]

Barclay got down to work immediately, and in January, 1812, he published his *Code on the Conduct of Major Military Operations,* a work more familiarly known as *The Yellow Book,* from the colour of its jacket. According to *The Yellow Book* the commander of the main army was directly responsible to the Tsar for carrying out the plan of 'major operations' which had been given to him. Inside the army the commander had the support of a headquarters which was composed of four 'directions' (general staff, artillery, engineering and commissariat). Headquarters were set up on the same lines at corps and divisional level. The staff officers were given a much-needed increase in authority and in return they

49

were expected to have at their fingertips the order of the army's business and the manner in which its movements were to be carried out.

In most aspects, therefore, the Russian army of 1812 could consider itself a worthy opponent of the *Grande Armée*. Its morale was high, its affairs were well regulated, and its tactics were well up with the times. The misfortunes of 1805-07 were safely in the past and had provided some useful lessons. The recent experience of the army had been in smallish wars which were instructive without being unduly destructive. Barclay and many other generals of 1812 had had a 'good war' in the campaigns against Sweden in 1808-09, which had resulted in the annexation of Finland. Since 1806 further Russian armies had been campaigning on the Danube against the Turks, a war which was to throw into prominence Field Marshal Kutuzov, a commander of whom we shall hear a good deal more.

Chapter 5

THE INVASION

Napoleon's invasion of Russia probably constituted the largest and most ambitious operation yet devised in the history of warfare. He laid the *Schwerpunkt* of his blow along the most direct route to Moscow, which led north of the Pripet Marshes. Under his immediate command he had a main army consisting of the Imperial Guard, Davout's I Corps and Ney's III Corps, and the two reserve cavalry corps of Nansouty and Montbrun. To the south-west was arrayed the Army of Italy under his stepson, Prince Eugène de Beauharnais, while the Emperor's brother Jérôme and his Second Support Army of Germans and Saxons closed up the flank. The right wing of the *Grande Armée* was therefore very much a family concern.

Detached forces were thrown out to either side of the main body. On the immediate left Marshal Oudinot with the 40,000 or so men of II Corps advanced against the middle Dvina. The important fortress-port of Riga, which stood at the mouth of the river, was the target of the Prussian auxiliary corps. South of the Pripet Marshes and on the extreme right of the invasion force was the 34,000-strong corps of Napoleon's unwilling allies, the Austrians, commanded by Prince Schwarzenberg.

All told, about 500,000 men of the *Grande Armée* and the flanking forces entered Russia in the course of the campaign. A further 175,000 remained in support in Poland and Eastern Germany.

At this stage it is only for convenience that we talk about 'the invasion of Russia' or 'the road to Moscow'. When Napoleon first went into Russia he only intended to bring Alexander to reason by catching and defeating the scattered Russian forces somewhere in the frontier region; he had no intention of conquering and ruling Muscovy. The odds were certainly in his favour at the outset, and there was every prospect of a rapid victory if he could get all the elements of the

51

Grande Armée of 1812 to move with anything like the harmony and speed his troops had shown in 1805.

The approach of the crisis found the Russians in considerable disarray. Despite every effort on the part of the Tsar's government the Russians were incapable of meeting Napoleon in anything like adequate force. In March, 1812, the Supply Army (118,000 men) and the recruits in the depôts (60,000) were mobilized as reserves, and in June some of these raw troops went to form six new infantry regiments. Eight regiments of line infantry and four of jaegers had already been set up in May. Latent in the provinces was the organization of the *opolchenie* (militia), which had been created in November, 1806, with the intention of giving the rudiments of military training to 612,000 of the peasants of private landowners. In the patriotic fervour of 1812 the *opolchenie* was opened to all comers, and 223,361 men were actually raised in the year. Russian historians variously reckon the size of the active army at the outbreak of hostilities in 1812 at between 518,000 and 815,000. Thus the Tsar could place well over a million men under arms, when one includes the cossacks and the *opolchenie*. But the Russians were unable to put more than a fraction of this force into the field at the beginning of the campaign. Not to mention the difficulty of raising the reserves, the high command had to commit many of its precious regulars to peripheral theatres: 24,000 troops kept watch on the ragged tribesmen of the Caucasus; 19,500 more were marooned in the Crimea, and 30,000 were stationed in Finland, recently conquered from the Swedes. On the Danube a peace had been hastily patched up with the Turks, but Admiral Chichagov and the 35,000-strong Army of Moldavia could not march from the Balkans in time for the opening of the new war in the north.

One might have expected the Russians to concentrate their forces at Vitebsk or Minsk, or in some reasonably central position from where they would be well placed to move against all the likely avenues of Napoleon's advance. Instead they split their troops into three isolated groups. Barclay was put in charge of a First West Army (made up of II, III and IV Corps – between 90,000 and 127,000 men) which assembled along the Niemen in front of the headquarters at Vilna. VI

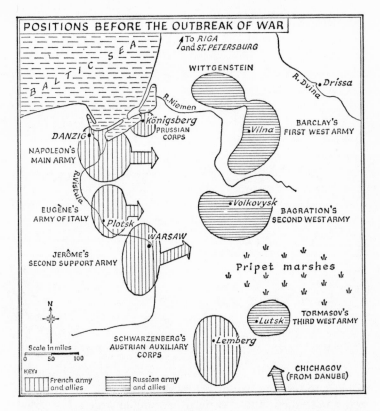

POSITIONS BEFORE THE OUTBREAK OF WAR

To *RIGA*
and *ST. PETERSBURG*

WITTGENSTEIN

R. Dvina • *Drissa*

R. Niemen

Königsberg
PRUSSIAN
CORPS

BARCLAY'S
FIRST WEST ARMY

Vilna

DANZIG •

NAPOLEON'S
MAIN ARMY

R. Vistula

EUGÈNE'S
ARMY OF ITALY

Plotsk

• *Volkovysk*

BAGRATION'S
SECOND WEST ARMY

WARSAW

JERÔME'S
SECOND SUPPORT ARMY

Pripet   marshes

N

TORMASOV'S
THIRD WEST ARMY

• *Lutsk*

Scale in miles

0   50   100

SCHWARZENBERG'S
AUSTRIAN AUXILIARY
CORPS

• *Lemberg*

CHICHAGOV
(FROM DANUBE)

KEY:

French army
and allies

Russian army
and allies

Corps and III Cavalry Corps kept up a tenuous communication
with the other main grouping, Prince Bagration's Second
West Army, consisting of about 60,000 men stationed to the
south around Volkovysk (VII and VIII Corps and IV Cavalry
Corps). General Tormasov and his Third West Army (45,000)
hardly come into the reckoning, as they were posted south of
the Pripet Marshes to keep watch on the Austrians.

This dispersion allowed Napoleon to drive between Barclay
and Bagration and penetrate the right centre of the 380-mile
Russian cordon.

What was the thinking behind these strange dispositions?
Amid the conflicting voices offering the Tsar advice Alexander
was most impressed by the calm and seemingly authoritative
Prussian colonel, Ernst von Phull, 'a peculiar mixture of men:

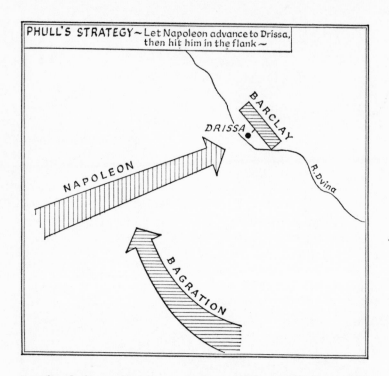

PHULL'S STRATEGY ~ Let Napoleon advance to Drissa, then hit him in the flank ~

BARCLAY

DRISSA

R. Dvina

NAPOLEON

BAGRATION

a melancholy meditator, a crank, a pedant and a complete stranger to the real world. He lived instead in a world of his own imagination, and contrived to stumble over every straw that lay athwart his path'.[1] The Tsar was much taken with the style of this strange young man, and he frequently invited him to his study to read out his immaculately reasoned expositions of strategy and military history.

Phull in turn was under the spell of the writings of his fellow-countryman Dietrich von Bülow, who had written a book (*Geist des neueren Kriegssystems*, 1799) which tried to reduce warfare to the status of a predictive science. (The United States was to know many people of the same kind in the 1960's.) From Bülow's famous theory of 'the line of operations' Phull deduced the strategy of drawing Napoleon onto either the First or Second West Army. The army in question was supposed to fall back to some advantageous position, and while the French raged impotently outside the

54

defences the other army would fall on the enemy communications. As a refuge for Barclay, if he came under attack, Phull designated the entrenched camp which was being built on the middle Dvina at Drissa. Phull was unconcerned by the fact that a retreat in this direction would pull Barclay north-eastwards and further away than ever from Bagration's army.

Barclay, the object of these scientific meditations, was meanwhile spending a wretched time at Vilna. While keeping the post of War Minister, he was put in nominal command of Bagration and other generals who were senior to him. He owned just enough authority to make himself thoroughly unpopular, but Alexander withheld the title of commander-in-chief and succeeded in destroying Barclay's remaining credit by coming out to Vilna with the Imperial suite. All urgency was lost in the round of festivities and pointless debates. 'The press there was huge. Everyone wanted to attract attention and make himself important. Suggestions and plans of campaign showered in from all sides, and Barclay needed all his equanimity not to lose his head amid all the new projects and the intrigues which were already on foot against him.'[2] His own inclination was to avoid a general battle and draw out the war as long as possible.

Among Barclay's rivals were Duke Alexander of Württemburg, the brutal and ambitious Lieutenant-General Ermolov, and the Grand Duke Constantine, an idle man who was nevertheless reckoned to be 'the very incarnation of the army's spirit of xenophobia and blind patriotism'.[3] The formidable Arakcheev himself emerged from obscurity and hung constantly about Alexander. In these circumstances nobody knew whether such and such a statement emanated from the Tsar or simply represented the opinion of the last person who had spoken.

Socially the low-born Barclay was outshone by another of his enemies, the senior general, von Bennigsen, who owned large estates in the neighbourhood of Vilna and was in a position to entertain on a royal scale. Among other enterprises he had a luxurious ballroom built in great haste at his mansion at Zakrety. Barclay would have been inhuman if he

55

had not felt a little satisfaction when the pavilion collapsed on the morning before the opening ball.

Carrying all their intrigues and jealousies with them, the Russian army and court decamped from Vilna when Napoleon's army crossed the frontier in the last week of June. True to Phull's plan, the First Army fell back on Drissa, where it arrived on 10 and 11 July. To everyone's horror the camp proved to be badly sited and far too cramped to accommodate the troops. 'The Tsar was crestfallen and his eyes brimmed with tears. We had to give up any thought of making a stand on this ground, and we had to work out a completely new strategy. Now we saw that the tide of war would roll over the Russian provinces.'[4]

A small party of elder statesmen, led by Arakcheev and the secretary of state Shishkov, soon persuaded the Tsar that his true place was in the interior of Russia, where he could help to mobilize the nation's resources. Alexander duly left Polotsk on 19 July, clutching a fine proclamation that had been penned by Shishkov, and on the 27th he met the aristocracy in Moscow and persuaded them to accept an unlimited increase in the *opolchenie*. The Tsar declared that he would never make peace with Napoleon 'as long as a single Frenchman stands on Russian soil'. The nobility and merchants sent in voluntary contributions of money, supplies and horses, and the Ukraine and the region of the Don raised almost 30,000 extra cossacks on their own initiative. Less welcome was the hatred which many native Russians began to harbour towards officers with foreign-sounding names, no matter how long these men or their ancestors had served their adopted country.

At the headquarters of the First Army everything seemed to have changed for the better after Alexander's departure. In an instant Barclay's deserted antechamber was 'filled again with the same people who had recently criticized him so bitterly. Barclay, cool and composed as always, betrayed not the slightest change in his conduct and treated his rivals with the same courtesy as before.'[5]

The first task was to extricate the Russian armies from their perilous position and combine them in a single force which could hold the field against the French. It was unfortunate that the two West Armies were kept apart not just by distance but by the characters of their commanders. Everything combined to set Barclay, the man of the Baltic, at odds with the commander of the Second West Army, Prince Bagration, the descendant of Georgian princes, with his swarthy features, flashing eyes and aquiline nose. 'On the one side', wrote Ségur, 'we have the cool courage and the informed, methodical and tenacious intelligence of Barclay; he had a German mind, as well as German blood, and he wished to reduce everything, even risks, to the process of calculation. On the other side we encounter the warlike, bold and violent instincts of Bagration, an out-and-out Russian of the school of Suvorov, who was unhappy at having to obey a general who was his junior. Bagration was terrible in combat, but he read in no other book save the one of nature. He was devoid of education, except for his own experiences, and he took counsel only of his impulses.'[6]

The purposeless move to Drissa had widened the gap between the West Armies, and Barclay therefore lost no time in striking south-east to regain communication with Smolensk and Moscow. On the right flank, General Wittgenstein and 25,000 men were left behind to cover the road to St Petersburg, while 14,000 troops remained on the coast to defend Riga. Barclay reached Vitebsk on 20 July, safely ahead of the *Grande Armée,* and stood his ground in the expectation that Bagration would cut up from the south by way of Mohilev and Orsha. He reckoned without Bagration's unwillingness to effect the union, and the very real difficulty he experienced in extricating himself from the clutches of the French.

For a time Bagration stood in danger of being driven into the Pripet Marshes by the right wing of the *Grande Armée.* He was saved by the slowness of Jérôme and the Second Support Army, which did nothing to take advantage of a shrewd move by Marshal Davout, who directed his I Corps through Minsk against Bagration's communications. Thus Bagration was free to escape from the pincers (Jérôme from the west, Davout from the north) by taking a diversion to the south and passing the Berezina at the fortified bridgehead of Bobruisk. Jérôme retired to his kingdom of Westphalia, smarting at Napoleon's criticisms, but the unfailingly efficient Davout pushed I Corps on to Mohilev, where he repulsed an attempt by Bagration to break through to the north on 23 July.

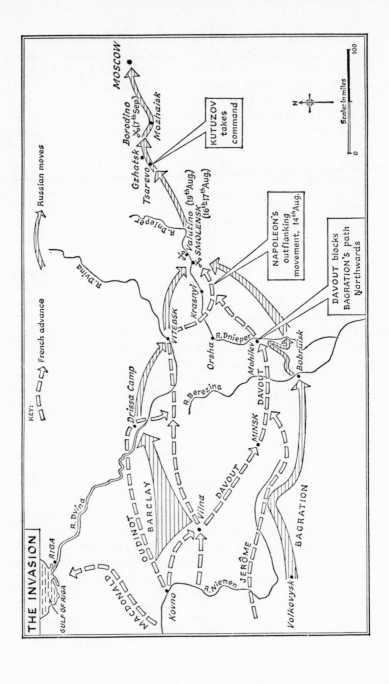

THE INVASION

MOSCOW

Borodino ✕(7th Sep.)
Mozhaisk
Gzhatsk
Tsarevo

KUTUZOV takes command

R. Dnieper

Valutino (19th Aug.)
SMOLENSK (16th-17th Aug.)

NAPOLEON'S outflanking movement, 14th Aug.

VITEBSK
Krasnyi
Orsha
R. Dnieper
Mohilev
DAVOUT
Bobruisk

DAVOUT blocks BAGRATION'S path Northwards

Drissa Camp

R. Berezina

MINSK

DAVOUT

R. Dvina

KEY:
╌╌╌⟩ French advance
⟹ Russian moves

OUDINOT

BARCLAY

Wilna

DAVOUT

JERÔME

R. Niemen

BAGRATION

Volkovysk

Kovno

RIGA
R. Dvina

MACDONALD

GULF OF RIGA

N

Scale: in miles
0   100

Barclay was preparing to do battle at Vitebsk when an adjutant arrived from Bagration with the news that the French were firmly ensconced on the Mohilev–Orsha–Vitebsk road. Barclay knew that his own army would almost certainly be overrun by Napoleon if he stood any longer at Vitebsk without support, so he abandoned the position on the night of 27/28 July, and the two Russian armies marched by converging courses on the city of Smolensk, where they united at the beginning of August.

The *Grande Armée* was also gradually coming together into one body as it crawled across the dusty plain in three parallel columns. IV Corps trailed after III Cavalry Corps to the left of the main force, while IV Cavalry Corps and V Corps took up a corresponding station on the far right. Between the two flanking forces marched the main body, which consisted of two corps of cavalry (I and II) and three of infantry (I, III and VIII). Veterans complained that the heat was as bad as in Egypt, and the dust was so thick that the sun was sometimes reduced to a dim red disc and drums had to be sounded at the head of every battalion to prevent the rear from losing its way.

In the centre of the army the broad, tree-lined Moscow road was left to the artillery and baggage, 'a bizarre confusion of every kind of carriage, team, individual and nag. There were vivandières, perched on wretched scraggy horses . . . there were soldiers, with knapsacks on their backs and muskets slung over their shoulders, mounted on donkeys or little local ponies whose legs were shorter than theirs.'[7]

In the lead rode the prancing, fantastic figure of Joachim Murat, King of Naples and commander of the advance guard of the *Grande Armée*. He looked as if he had just raided a theatrical wardrobe, with his great gold spurs, huge riding boots à la Gustavus Adolphus, his sumptuously-embroidered jacket of light blue, and his cascading black ringlets surmounted by a white-plumed Jacobean hat. An entire cart was given over exclusively to the transport of his perfumes, pomades and cosmetics. He was one of the foremost cavalry leaders of the time, and if he had all the appearances of a pantomime king he also owned some of the attributes of a real one.

Murat's cossack enemies loved him for his panache, and lived in hopes of taking him alive – not that they ever engaged

59

in serious combat with the advancing French cavalry. For day after day they hovered just in front of the advance guard, clearing and burning the villages as they went in a ruthless application of scorched-earth tactics. The first sign of the work of the incendiarists was usually 'a column of thick black smoke which climbed perpendicularly towards the sky then flowed away in the direction of the wind; thereupon other columns of the same kind welled up in succession and soon the flames would spread through the entire village, consuming it completely in less than a quarter of an hour.'[8]

Despite every appearance to the contrary, the campaigning of July represented for Napoleon a strategic defeat of the first order. Certainly he had demoralized the enemy by pushing them back to Smolensk, which stood inside the boundaries of ancient Muscovy, but he had failed to catch and destroy the individual Russian armies during the precious and irretrievable weeks when Barclay was still separated from Bagration. The trouble was that Napoleon had left out of account the relation between the availability of supplies and the speed of marching. For years now the French armies had been accustomed to 'living off the country', moving swiftly and unencumbered about the fertile face of western Europe. The forests and sandy plains of Russia were a different proposition, and Napoleon had to form supply convoys of thousands of waggons, which threw upon the transport services and the commissariat a burden which they had not shouldered since the 1790's. More than 20,000 horses had already been lost by the time Napoleon reached Vilna, and his armies dragged themselves along as if weighed down by ball and chain. The whole course of the campaign of 1812 can be seen as a progressive collapse of supply arrangements which began the moment the *Grande Armée* entered Russia.

All of this was of little immediate consolation to the dispirited Russians at Smolensk. Barclay was being severely criticized for having abandoned so much of the soil of Holy Russia, and he tried to recoup some of his lost credit by hurling the First West Army at the scattered French forces resting in the region of Vitebsk. On 6 August Ataman Platov with the cossacks of the advance guard succeeded in mauling 3,000 French cavalry under General Sébastiani at Inkovo. It was rare for cossacks to score so heavily against regular cavalry, but this apparently auspicious start to the offensive was attended by two unfortunate effects. First it transpired from a captured letter that the French had had wind of Barclay's scheme, and the suspicions of the anti-foreign party were focused on the innocent Ludwig von Wolzogen, one of Barclay's tame Prussians. Secondly Barclay feared that the French might retaliate and so, instead of following up his advantage, he swung northwards away from the main concentration of the French forces. He was still marching and countermarching when, several days later, word came from Bagration that Smolensk stood in imminent danger.

Barclay's loss of nerve had given Napoleon time to organize a grand enveloping movement against Smolensk, and he brought 175,000 men in an anti-clockwise sweep across the Dnieper between Orsha and Krasnyi with the intention of turning Smolensk from the south. This splendid scheme was ruined by an almost ridiculous oversight – Napoleon had failed to notice that a little force of Russians was moving along the south bank of the Dnieper squarely in the path of the advance. Lieutenant-General Neverovsky had at hand just fifteen hundred cavalry and his own 27th Infantry Division of 8,000 mostly raw troops, but with this small band he contrived on 14 August to repulse the French advance guard and execute a fighting retreat along the road from Krasnyi to Smolensk. Neverovsky's action held up the French long enough to allow Barclay and Bagration to draw in their forces to the suburbs and the old city wall of Smolensk.

Now that he had failed for a second time to catch the Russians at a disadvantage, Napoleon lost patience and threw his army against Smolensk in a bloody frontal battle which lasted throughout 16 and 17 August. While Lieutenant-General Raevsky and a single corps manfully stood their ground at Smolensk, Barclay and Bagration worked out a scheme to disengage the main armies. Bagration was to leave first, and withdraw his army along the north bank of the Dnieper, taking care to leave behind parties to cover the fords. Bagration duly set off on the 17th, but he disappeared with such speed that a dangerous gap opened up between the Second West Army and the First, which did not leave Smolensk until the following

61

night. Worse still, Bagration had not taken the agreed precautions to guard the fords, so that on the 19th the corps of General Junot was able to splash across to the 'Russian' bank at the same time as the main French army closed in on the First West Army's rearguard. Barclay beat off the main French army in a bitter little action at Valutino, on the plateau east of Smolensk, and luckily for him Junot was moving so slowly that the First West Army was able to make good its escape along the Moscow road.

For the third time the Russians had evaded the *Grande Armée*'s pincer movements, and Napoleon halted at Smolensk to take stock of the situation. Sickness and desertion had thinned his army's ranks to 185,000 men by the time he reached Smolensk, and the heavy marching and fighting of the last few days had probably cost him over 25,000 more. Everything seemed to indicate that he ought to be content for the moment with the capture of Smolensk, and consolidate his forces behind the river lines of the Dvina and the Dnieper while he made ready for a new campaign in 1813. He had by now outrun his supply depôts, and 280 miles separated him from the next major town to the east, which was Moscow.

Nevertheless Napoleon decided to continue the advance and break Alexander's will by forcing a decisive battle and the French left Smolensk on 25 August. Providence gave Napoleon a chance to change his mind, in the shape of a couple of days of heavy rain which washed out the roads, but the Emperor ignored the hint and drove his army on to its ultimate destruction.

Chapter 6

KUTUZOV TAKES COMMAND

Barclay and Bagration were barely on speaking terms after the episodes of Inkovo and Valutino, and the apparently endless retreat had the effect of reviving all the talk about Barclay's 'mistakes' and 'cowardice'. There were appeals to the spirit of Suvorov, who, people said, would have been all for fighting instead of arguing and sticking pins in maps. Barclay persuaded the Tsar to recall Grand Duke Constantine, the worst of the trouble-makers, but the so-called National Party maintained its onslaughts on Barclay's 'German Headquarters' and in particular on Wolzogen, whom they pictured as 'a large poisonous spider' lurking in a corner of the commander's room.

The seemingly unresisted advance of the French had caused a sensation in Moscow, which was the centre of the old anti-court, xenophobic aristocracy. The nobles mobilized 'public opinion' in favour of a change of command, and thus, according to the patriotic commentator Glinka, 'the courageous, sonorous voice of the army was greeted by another note, still more resounding and exalted, the voice of Russia itself'.[1]

Old General Kutuzov was the one indisputably Russian commander who had the stature and prestige to take over the command from Barclay.

Mikhail Illarionovich Golenishchev-Kutuzov was born in St Petersburg on 11 September, 1745, to a family of the old nobility, one of whose members had fought alongside Alexander Nevsky, the hero of ancient Muscovy. Mikhail's father was an eminent military engineer; however, he entered the artillery arm in 1759, and passed a few years later into the new corps of jaegers. The first Russian jaegers were formed by Field-Marshal Rumyantsev in 1761 out of 'prime soldiers of the most fit and agile kind', who were trained to move 'across fields and woods rather than along roads'.[2] Kutuzov rose to become chief of the jaeger corps and led them with outstanding success in the wars against the Turks in the second half of the eighteenth century. His reputation was enhanced by the bizarre distinction of having been shot twice through the head with little apparent effect. In August, 1774, during the attack on the Turkish entrenched camp at Shumla, he was knocked down by a bullet which entered his left cheek and came out near the right eye. On 30 August, 1788, one of the garrison troops of the Turkish fortress of Ochakov sent a ball through his left cheek and out at the back of his neck. Long afterwards an eminent German surgeon examined the scars and pronounced that he must be talking to a dead man. Kutuzov picked himself up a second time and accompanied Suvorov to the heroic storm of Izmail in 1790. After the action Suvorov wrote that 'the courage of my worthy and stout Major-General Kutuzov was an example to his subordinates . . . he took up position on my left flank, but it would be true to say he was my right-hand man.'[3]

Kutuzov exercised nominal command of the Russian army at Austerlitz in 1805, though the Tsar and the Austrians overruled so much of his good advice on that fatal day that he escaped with his reputation intact. In 1811 he was summoned to take charge of the forces on the Danube, where a war against the Turks had been going on indecisively since 1806. He encircled and captured a Turkish army at Rushchuk in December, and because the Turks were still disinclined to make peace he pushed beyond the Danube in the following year and brought them to the conference table at Bucharest. Peace was signed on 28 May, 1812, and the Russians were at last free to move their troops from the Danube.

These signal services did nothing to endear Kutuzov to Alexander, who regarded him as 'a hatcher of intrigues and an immoral and thoroughly dangerous character'.[4] Alexander created Kutuzov a prince, as was only proper, but he took him away from the southern army and gave him the humble post of commander of the St Petersburg *opolchenie*.

There is a temptation (irresistible to some film-makers) to portray the old gentleman as an archetypal *muzhik*, sprung from the soil of Russia to be the salvation of his land. This interpretation may be rejected out of hand. Kutuzov possessed an infinitely experienced, infinitely subtle personality. Wilson found him 'polished, courteous, shrewd as a Greek, naturally intelligent as an Asiatic, and well-instructed as a European',[5] while Kutuzov's own chief-of-staff, Bennigsen, complained that his chief had lost the habit of mental work and was apt to be guided by whatever favourite had sway over him at the particular moment.

Perhaps the answer is that we are dealing with somebody who was living out of his time, and carried the habits of the eighteenth century into the passionate and intense era of the struggle against Napoleon. Kutuzov could move an army's heart, but he rarely spoke or acted without having weighed the effect beforehand; he would accept a fight with equanimity, when the occasion absolutely demanded it, but he appreciated the effect of time upon military operations much better than did most of his generals. His wig and his amply-filled waistcoat harked back to the commanders he had seen in the 1750's, and like the people of those times he contrived to live in considerable style even on campaign. Straight-laced foreigners were liable to be shocked at the raffish atmosphere which reigned at his headquarters, for Kutuzov allowed nothing to interfere with the indulgence of his appetites for champagne, fine food, easy women and bad French novels. It was entirely in keeping with the rest of his character that he conveyed his orders at Borodino in French, the international language of the time.

The physical effects of Kutuzov's age and habits were all too evident, and like Marshal de Saxe in 1745 he fought his last great campaign in a state of advanced bodily decay. He could ride only with some difficulty, and preferred to be hauled about in a little four-wheeled drozhki.

It was a letter from Rostopchin, the governor of Moscow, which brought home to the Tsar the strength of feeling in favour of Kutuzov. Much against his better judgment Alexander decided to put him in charge of the western armies, though he effected the actual transfer of power through the tactful means of a committee of military men and statesmen, which had been set up with the nominal purpose of securing a better working relationship between Barclay and Bagration. On 20 August Kutuzov was given formal authority over both West

Armies and Barclay reverted to the command of the First Army.

When Kutuzov went to the door of his house in St Petersburg on 23 August he came face to face with such a crowd that his staff had to go ahead to clear the way. On the road to the army he repeatedly halted to return the greetings of the peasants and townspeople, or chat with the various officers who had fallen out with Barclay and were on their way back to St Petersburg. Kutuzov made one of the greatest mistakes of his life when he persuaded one of these men, General Levin Bennigsen, to come back with him as his Chief-of-Staff. Bennigsen had been born in Hanover, but he managed to identify himself so completely with the National Party that he escaped the obloquy which was being heaped on the other foreigners. He had missed the chastening experience of Austerlitz, and had been rewarded with more praise than was good for him for his creditable but not at all brilliant handling of the Russian army at Eylau and Friedland in 1807. His fellow-German Wolzogen described him as being 'proud and most cunning, and a man who was steadfast in anything which had to do with the pursuit of his own intrigues. He was extremely enterprising, but he was blinkered by his habit of regarding everything only in the light of his private interests.'[6] It was too late when Kutuzov finally detected the vices of the man he had chosen to interpret his intentions to the army.

Kutuzov reached the army at Tsarevo on 29 August, 'accompanied by the blessings of all Russia and incorporating in himself the hopes of the entire state.'[7] One of his officers wrote that 'on the very same day that he arrived at Tsarevo he ordained everything as if he had been managing affairs since the beginning of the campaign. Nothing seemed unfamiliar to him. He had foreseen every eventuality, and he functioned as a commander in the full sense of the word.'[8] There had been some talk about failing eyesight, for the old general's right eye was milky-white and probably useless, but he promptly put his staff to shame by identifying a party of cossacks from a prodigious distance.

Kutuzov made all the noises appropriate to a man who had come with the reputation of a fighting general. 'How could anyone think of retreating with such lads!' he loudly exclaimed when he first reviewed the troops. At the same time he wrote to his anxious wife: 'God has kept me in good health, my dear, and I am full of confidence. The army is in splendid spirits and we have many good generals.'[9]

In his own mind Kutuzov was working out ways to reconcile the realities of the situation with the unspoken commission from the whole of Russia to smash the invaders. He was only too well aware that the loss of some ex-Polish provinces would be as nothing compared with the abandonment of 'our ancient capital of Moscow',[10] but he was taken aback by the battering which had reduced the two West Armies to 100,000 or 120,000 weary men, and he stood in desperate need of time to receive and incorporate reinforcements, which were supposed to amount to more than 100,000 regular troops and the same number of the *opolchenie*. Thus Kutuzov ordered the army to decamp from Tsarevo and continue the retreat along the Moscow road.

The army was fast outrunning the potential battle sites which had been selected by Barclay's staff officers, and the first retrograde step under Kutuzov's command brought the troops on the night of 30/31 August to Ivashkovo, near Gzhatsk, where Kutuzov and Barclay resigned themselves to giving battle. Bennigsen, however, claimed that he had seen a splendid site from his carriage when he was travelling through Borodino, which was near Mozhaisk about twenty-five miles further east, and it was entirely on the strength of his arguments that Kutuzov ordered the army to pick itself up again and resume the retreat.

Kutuzov wrote circumspectly to the Tsar on the 31st that 'things being as they are I shall give battle to save Moscow, though I shall undertake the combat with every precaution demanded by the issue at stake'.[11] On the same day he informed General Tormasov that the battle would be staged somewhere in the region of Mozhaisk. Thus Kutuzov announced his decision to fight, while cunningly reconciling Alexander and the generals to the necessity of falling back just a little bit more. Needless to say the continual halting and marching threw a heavy responsibility on the commander of the rear-guard, Lieutenant-General Konovnitsyn, 'a kindly, expert and brave kind of person',[12] who had taken over at Vyazma from the temperamental cossack ataman Platov. Konovnitsyn's little band staged bitter actions with the French advance guard at Gzhatsk, at the wood of Gridnevo, and lastly around the Kolotskoi Monastery near Borodino.

All the time Kutuzov bombarded Governor Rostopchin with requests for reinforcements, food and fodder, and he did not forget to ask him to send F. Leppich's famous observation balloon to the army as well. The response was grievously disappointing. The only regular troops who turned up were 15,589 mostly green recruits led by General Miloradovich. For the rest Kutuzov had to make what use he could of the 15,000 or so Moscow and Smolensk *opolchenie,* 'raw Russian peasants clutching pikes and muskets which they scarcely knew how to wield.'[13]

It was too late for second thoughts now that Kutuzov was committed to battle. On the morning of 3 September the army marched from the Kolotskoi Monastery to the little valleys and low rounded hills which encircled the village of Borodino, on the borders of the Government of Moscow and about seventy miles from the capital itself. Denis Davydov's family owned land in the district, and he had 'more reason to be familiar with those fields and that village than did the rest of the army. It was there that I spent the carefree years of my childhood, and my heart was first impelled towards love and glory. But what a sight the cradle of my youth now presented! My family house was hidden by the smoke of the camp fires, rows of bayonets glittered among the helmets of the cavalry, and troops were massing among my native hills and valleys. There, on a mound where I used to play, they were throwing up the Raevsky Redoubt. The pretty little wood in front had been hewn down to form an abattis and it was now swarming with jaegers. The village was already deserted by its inhabitants, though one of the men was wandering with his wife among the troops who had ransacked his kitchen garden: he knew I was in the army and he wished to track me down. I gave him some money, but what he really wanted was bread ... That day was among the cruellest of my life.'[14]

Davydov was not left to brood overlong, for Bagration sent him towards the Kolotskoi Monastery, where Konovnitsyn was executing a fighting retreat with the rearguard. 'As I rode the several miles to the monastery the combat in the valley was gradually unfolded to my view. The enemy was breaking through with all his force. The roar of the guns was continuous, and their smoke mingled with the smoke of the fires to cover the whole neighbourhood was a kind of mist.'[15]

The French reached the Kolotskoi Monastery with their confidence unabated. The dreadful heat of the last weeks had been broken by a rainstorm on 30 August, and on the 31st, which dawned fine but refreshing, Napoleon learnt from a captured cossack that Kutuzov had taken command of the Russians. The Emperor was doubly delighted: he was unimpressed by what he knew of Kutuzov's performance in the campaign of Austerlitz in 1805, and he was confident that Kutuzov was under pressure to bring on a 'good battle' which would give the *Grande Armée* the chance to finish the war there and then. Napoleon's troops reached Gzhatsk on 1 September, and after a full two days' rest they pressed on to arrive within view of the Russian army on the 5th.

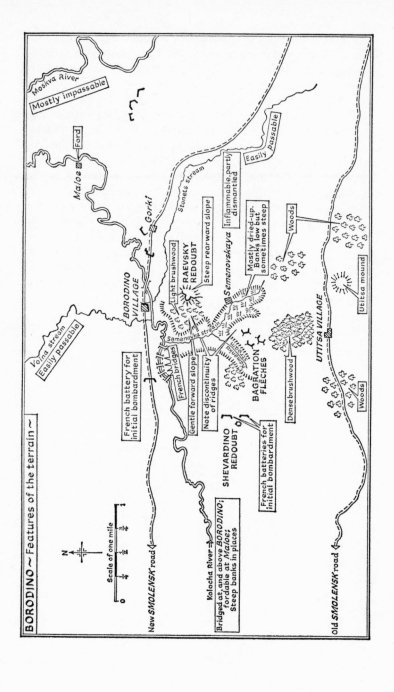

BORODINO ~ Features of the terrain ~

Moskva River
Mostly impassable

Ford
Maloe

Gorki

Stonets stream

BORODINO VILLAGE

Light brushwood

RAEVSKY REDOUBT

Steep rearward slope

Semenovskaya

Inflammable, partly dismantled

Mostly dried-up. Banks low but sometimes steep

Woods

Utitsa mound

UTITSA VILLAGE

Semenovska stream

Voina stream
Easily passable

French battery for initial bombardment

French bridges

Gentle forward slope

Note discontinuity of ridges

Brushwood

BAGRATION FLÈCHES

Dense brushwood

Woods

SHEVARDINO REDOUBT

French batteries for initial bombardment

N

Scale of one mile

New SMOLENSK road

Kolocha River
Bridged at, and above BORODINO; fordable at Maloe; Steep banks in places

Old SMOLENSK road

Chapter 7

MAKING READY FOR THE BATTLE

Kutuzov toured the battle site on 3 September, accompanied by a huge eagle which wheeled over him wherever he went. Russian (and Austrian) armies were usually favoured with such omens before a successful fight, and the troops at Borodino were suitably impressed. For the moment, however, Kutuzov was doing little more than confirming the recommendations of Lieutenant-Colonel Harting, a staff officer who had been sent ahead by Bennigsen on 1 September to make a detailed reconnaissance.

The chosen field stretched across beautiful rolling countryside broken here and there by copses or larger woods of birch and pine. The position had the strategic advantage of lying between the two routes to Moscow, the Old and the New Smolensk Roads, which ran east on converging courses to unite at Mozhaisk, behind the battlefield. The road continued on to Moscow through a vast tract of forest.

The right (northern) flank of the line was covered by the steep banks of the Kolocha stream which ran in a generally south-west to north-east direction towards the Moskva River. Twenty-six guns were now sited in a chain of fortifications behind the Kolocha, and twelve further pieces (heavy ones) were mounted in two batteries which were disposed, one behind the other, just to the north of the New Smolensk Road near Gorki.

The southern flank of the right wing rested in the area where the little streams Voina, Kamenka, Semenovka and Stonets converged upon the Kolocha like the spokes of a wheel. The village of Borodino stood almost at the hub, in the angle formed by the confluence of the Voina and the Kolocha. Unfortunately for the Russians, the Kolocha cut off the position of the main army from the village, which lessened its defensive value. Kutuzov instead made his stand on the east

71

bank of the river, where he could take advantage of a low and discontinuous ridge.

At the northern end of the ridge and several hundred yards back from the confluence of the Kolocha and the Semenovka there was a mound which commanded a magnificent field of fire. Colonel Carl von Toll, a staff officer, was the first to appreciate the potentialities of the site, and on his advice Kutuzov planted a strong battery of eighteen twelve-pounder cannon on the summit. This work was to become famous in military history as 'The Raevsky Redoubt'.

As originally constructed, the fortification consisted of two short sideways-facing *épaulements,* and two long forward-slanting parapets which met in a 'V' of 160 degrees. The work was open to the rear (and so at this stage could not properly be called a 'redoubt'), and it owned no protection on the forward side except for a shallow twenty-two-foot wide ditch. The arc of fire was designed to interlock with the arcs of the batteries near Gorki, and the ground in front fell away towards the Semenovka in a natural glacis which enabled the gunners to attain the full 'razing effect' with their shot.

Barclay's First West Army was given the task of holding the right wing and his force was more than adequate for the purpose. He had Platov's cossacks and I Cavalry Corps (Uvarov) tucked away as a mobile reserve behind the right flank, while II (Baggovut) and IV (Ostermann-Tolstoy) Corps were deployed in the almost invulnerable positions behind the Kolocha. VI Corps (Dokhturov) occupied the ground as far as the Raevsky Redoubt, though the defence of the redoubt itself was entrusted to Paskevich's division of VII Corps (Raevsky), a force which really belonged to the Second Army. II (Korff) and III (Kreutz) Cavalry Corps stood in immediate support behind the infantry. Ahead of the main army the Lifeguard Jaegers were ensconced in Borodino village on the far side of the Kolocha. In concentrating so much of his force on the right wing, which was the least accessible sector of the position, Kutuzov seems to have been influenced by the belief that the French would make their effort along the axis of the New Smolensk Road.

By comparison Bagration's sector on the centre and left was much more vulnerable. South of the Raevsky Redoubt

72

there was a stretch of about 2,500 yards which owned no protection except for the marshy banks and stagnant pools of the Semenovka stream. The village of Semenovskaya occupied a key position on the east bank, but its wooden houses were useless for defence and the Russians were forced to take them to pieces or burn them down.

The left flank of the Second Army proper was closed up by a trio of three 'V'-shaped fortifications, the 'Bagration Flèches', which gave a badly-needed accession of strength. A further earthwork, the Shevardino Redoubt, stood forlornly in the plain a mile in front of the Bagration Flèches. It had been built on the suggestion of Colonel Toll as a defensible observation post from which to 'discover the direction in which the French were pushing their forces and, if possible, divine what Napoleon was aiming at'.[1]

General Raevsky's VII Corps had the heavy responsibility of holding the Raevsky Redoubt and the line as far south as the site of the village of Semenovskaya, with IV Cavalry Corps (Sievers) in support. Vorontsov's 7th Combined Grenadier Division was brought into the Bagration Flèches, and the gallant Neverovsky stationed his 27th Infantry Division behind: these forces came under Lieutenant-General Borozdin, overall commander of VIII Corps.

Kutuzov positioned a powerful force in the centre rear as a general reserve, to be available to both his armies. This consisted of the 1st and 2nd Cuirassier Divisions, Lavrov's Lifeguard Infantry Division (together making up V Corps) and Tuchkov's III Corps. The artillery reserve of twenty-six batteries (300 pieces with 8,400 gunners) was assembled in the area of Psarevo. Most of the *opolchenie* were distributed in a chain behind the regular forces. They were under orders to carry away the wounded and intercept deserters, and Kutuzov hoped that they would deceive the French into thinking he had powerful additional reserves arrayed in his rear.

Kutuzov was oddly slow to appreciate the possibility that the French might push around his left flank by way of the Old Smolensk Road. He reported afterwards to Alexander that 'the French came into sight on 6 September (actually it was the 5th). The enemy threw up some fortifications in advance of their front, and on their right flank we could make out some movements, partly hidden from us by the woods, from which we deduced that Napoleon intended to launch an attack on our left flank and then, by continuing his advance along the Old Smolensk Road, cut us off from Mozhaisk.'[2] This build-up of forces presaged the attack on the Shevardino Redoubt (see below pp. 77–80). On the evening of the 5th Kutuzov accordingly detached the 8,000 men of Tuchkov's III Corps from the reserve and sent them with 1,500 cossacks and 7,000 of the Moscow *opolchenie* to cover the Old Smolensk Road in the region of the village of Utitsa.

Kutuzov did not attempt to fortify the prehistoric Utitsa Mound which rose up behind the village, but arranged Tuchkov's command under cover of thick woods in a kind of giant ambush. The site was expertly selected by the engineer, Captain Felker, and Kutuzov hoped that 'when the enemy commit their last reserves against Bagration's left flank, I shall be able to strike them in the flank and rear with my concealed forces'.[3] To the north-west of the ambush the 20th, 21st, 11th and 41st Jaeger Regiments were deployed in the area of lighter secondary growth which extended for about a mile to the left wing of Bagration's Second West Army.

As ill-luck had it, General Bennigsen drove through the area in his drozhki on the 6th and leant a willing ear to the complaints of the jaegers, who were nervous about being so isolated. He therefore went on to Tuchkov, and ordered him to leave his hidden position and advance into open ground so as to close up with the jaegers. A young staff officer, Ensign Shcherbinin, was watching the episode with silent interest. He was in on the secret of the original stratagem, but he assumed that such a drastic change in the arrangements must have been approved by Kutuzov himself. Next year Shcherbinin was chatting with Colonel Toll over tea and took the opportunity to ask him why Kutuzov had changed his mind. At this Toll burst out: 'It was not a question of His Highness changing his mind. There must have been some mistake in the way the orders were carried out.'[4] Toll got up, wound himself about with his sash (for Kutuzov was a stickler for appearances) and stumped off to headquarters to take up the matter with the commander-in-chief. Like everyone else Kutuzov had assumed

74

that the muddle on the left had been the responsibility of Tuchkov, who was killed on the 7th. He was enraged to find that the fault was Bennigsen's after all, and he told Colonel Toll that it was entirely in keeping with what he knew of Bennigsen's wilful ways. Shcherbinin nevertheless points out that Kutuzov ought to have taken Bennigsen into his confidence from the beginning, and that the misunderstanding showed 'how dangerous it is for a commander-in-chief to conceal his arrangements from his chief-of-staff. Unfortunately Kutuzov was a general of the old school, and he had not read deeply enough in *The Yellow Book,* which contains our rules for managing the army'.[5]

It was probably for the same reason that the command of the Russian forces was divided in a haphazard manner between the levels of corps and army. On the right General Miloradovich was in charge of II and IV Corps and the cavalrymen of Uvarov and Korff. Prince Gorchakov had another large command, comprising VII and VIII Corps and Sievers' cavalry, which made up practically the whole of the Second West Army. In contrast Dokhturov in the centre commanded only his own VI Corps and III Cavalry Corps. Grand Duke Constantine led the reserve.

To sum up, the Russian Army at Borodino was divided into a right wing which was almost too strong, and a left wing which was over-extended and vulnerable. Tuchkov's command on the extreme left was particularly exposed after Bennigsen had done his work. Undeterred, Kutuzov wrote exultantly to the Tsar that 'the position I have taken up at Borodino four miles from Mozhaisk is one of the best you could find in this rather weak terrain. I have resorted to artifice in order to remedy the one weak sector of the line, which lies on the left. I only hope the enemy will attack us in our position: if they do, I am confident we shall win.'[6]

The Russian array certainly looked impressive enough from where the French were standing. One of Napoleon's Germans, the Saxon dragoon officer von Leissnig, swept the field with his telescope. 'As far as my inquisitive eye could see the whole ground to the left and right and straight ahead was covered with a growth of hazel bushes, junipers and other brushwood which rose to at least a man's height. To the left

75

centre, about two thousand paces distant, stood a village (Borodino) and a nice Byzantine church which rose from a gentle tree-covered slope and had a pretty tower plated in green copper.' To the right he could make out a ridge 'covered along almost all its length with masses of Russian infantry and artillery. As I could clearly see through my telescope the Russians had thrown up earthworks on some of the highest points of the ridge. These fortifications were cut into notches which seemed to be the embrasures for the artillery. Obliquely to the right of our regiment and beyond the ridge there rose the towers of the churches of Mozhaisk and the nearby monastery. They were an hour's march away, but they succeeded in lending a touch of beauty to the brooding gloom of the wild and barren neighbourhood'.[7]

Russian officers at all levels of seniority could not imagine why Kutuzov had piled up so many forces on the right at the expense of the left. The artillery officer, Rodozhitsky, strolled over the field with his friend, Captain Figner, who pointed out that in past actions Napoleon had consistently concentrated his troops against the left wing of the Russian army. ' "Mark my words", he said, "Napoleon will throw all his forces on this flank and drive us into the River Moskva." '[8] According to General Ermolov 'the left wing was tangibly weak in comparison with the other sectors of our position. The fortifications there were insignificant, and time was so short that there was nothing we could do to strengthen them.'[9] He tells us that on the 6th Bennigsen proposed to leave a thin cordon of jaegers along the right, and bring II and IV Corps south to act as a reserve to Bagration. On the same evening Barclay advanced the still more drastic solution of shifting the combined armies bodily to the left, so that Bagration's left flank would come to rest around Utitsa. Kutuzov nodded approvingly to both suggestions, but he did nothing about putting them into effect.

In striking contrast with the cunning habits of their great contemporary Wellington, who liked to hide his forces behind folds in the ground, the Russians at Borodino put all their troops 'in the shop window' in full view of the French. The jaeger regiments of the infantry divisions were spread out nearest the enemy along the river banks and in the brushwood.

Next came the line infantry, arrayed in two rows of battalion columns (dense formations in themselves) with the cavalry deployed in two lines in close support. The local and general reserves stood almost immediately behind, in accordance with the order 'to have them as close as possible to the fortifications'.[10] Thousands of men lost their lives to no purpose because the French gunners had such excellent targets in those compact masses of troops standing motionless in the open. Thus the Preobrazhensky and Semenovsky Lifeguards, in reserve, still 'suffered heavy casualties without having had the chance to give a musket shot in reply'.[11]

Yet again we may trace the handiwork of Bennigsen, the Chief-of-Staff. Wolzogen protested against his murderous arrangements, but Bennigsen replied that the 'deep and compact order of battle is the best means to avoid being crushed by Napoleon, who usually confines his attack to the centre of the enemy army'.[12]

All the time Napoleon was slowly bringing his troops forward and building up a massive concentration of force south of the Kolocha against the Russian left wing. Early in the afternoon of 5 September he rode out to see what the Russians were doing around the Shevardino Redoubt—it was not much of an obstacle in itself, but it hindered him from deploying his right wing. After an attentive study of the ground through his telescope he 'began to hum an insignificant tune',[13] then spoke briefly with Murat and rode off to arrange the plan of attack. The French army was meanwhile unrolling in immense columns, watched by the silent Russian battalions. Eighteen thousand Russians were grouped around the redoubt itself. General Neverovsky's 27th Infantry Division had advanced from the Bagration Flèches and was standing just behind the work. Three jaeger regiments were thrown out in a long chain to either side, and powerful detachments of cavalry were positioned in close support.

Napoleon ordered Poniatowski's V Corps of Poles to undertake a flanking sweep through the wooded terrain to the south, but he entrusted the direct attack on the redoubt to Compans' division of I Corps. Compans' troops moved off in battalion columns in the late afternoon, followed by the two cavalry corps of Nansouty and Montbrun. An eyewitness

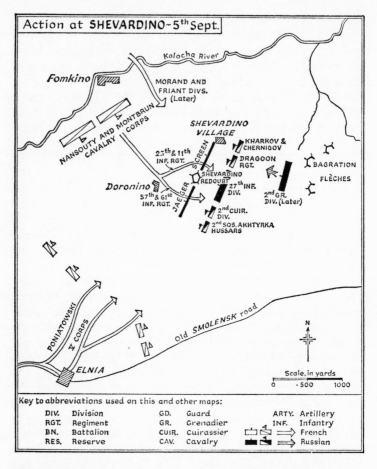

Action at SHEVARDINO~5th Sept.

Kolocha River

Fomkino

MORAND AND
FRIANT DIVS.
(Later)

NANSOUTY AND MONTBRUN
CAVALRY CORPS

SHEVARDINO
VILLAGE

KHARKOV &
CHERNIGOV

25th & 11th
INF. RGT.

DRAGOON
RGT.

JAEGER SCREEN

SHEVARDINO
REDOUBT

BAGRATION

FLÈCHES

Doronino

27th INF.
DIV.

57th & 61st
INF. RGT.

2nd GR.
DIV. (Later)

2nd CUIR.
DIV.

2nd SQS. AKHTYRKA
HUSSARS

PONIATOWSKI V CORPS

Old SMOLENSK road

N

ELNIA

Scale, in yards
0   500   1000

Key to abbreviations used on this and other maps:

DIV.	Division	GD.	Guard	ARTY.	Artillery
RGT.	Regiment	GR.	Grenadier	INF.	Infantry
BN.	Battalion	CUIR.	Cuirassier		French
RES.	Reserve	CAV.	Cavalry		Russian

recalls that 'it was wonderful to see the keenness of our troops.
The beauty of the scene was enhanced by the splendid sky
and by the setting sun which was reflected from the muskets
and sabres. From its positions the rest of the army watched
the troops as they marched on, proud to have been chosen as
the first to come to grips with the enemy.'[14]

Preceded by a cloud of skirmishers, Compans' division
advanced by way of Fomkino and Doronino and pushed back
the Russian light infantry. Compans twice unlimbered a
powerful battery of artillery, the first time on high ground at

Fomkino then again at a murderously short distance where the effect of the gunfire was seconded by six or seven companies of *voltigeurs,* who grouped themselves on a small mound and peppered the Russian garrison at a range of 120 paces.

Such was the noisy prelude to an 'encounter battle' which was fought under conditions of fading light and darkness. The commander of the artillery of the Russian Second West Army, Major-General Waldemar von Löwenstern, so misread the situation that he rode off to make a glowing report to Bagration on the performance of the gunners in the redoubt. He returned to find that the artillery and some of the covering infantry were streaming away from the site. Hastily revising his ideas, he summoned up a further battery and committed a brigade of the 27th Infantry Division to the struggle. These reinforcements recovered the battery for the Russians. A point-blank musketry duel ensued between the 27th Division and the French infantry, who were lapping around on both sides – the 25th and 11th Regiments to the left of the redoubt, and the 57th and 61st to the south. The bloody and indecisive contest lasted until, after three quarters of an hour, Compans brought up four guns behind the cover of the 57th Regiment and discharged them straight into the compact green ranks of the Russian infantry, upon which the 57th pushed the shattered Russians back at bayonet point, and the 61st swept into the redoubt where they found that 'gunners, horses, every living thing had been destroyed by the fire of our *voltigeurs*'.[15]

The action around the Shevardino Redoubt was fast becoming a general battle between the southern wings of the rival armies. Prince Gorchakov fed the 2nd Grenadier Division into the fight and recaptured the corpse-strewn battery for a second time. On the French side the cavalry of Nansouty and Montbrun were closing up with the French infantry and sweeping the plain. The Russian grenadiers held on in the redoubt only with great difficulty, and Gorchakov admits that he 'wanted nothing better than for night to fall and bring an end to the battle'. Soon he heard 'the loud tramping of enemy horses. The night was already so dark that it was impossible to make out the number, though from the sound alone it was clear that the enemy were cavalry and that they were coming on in fairly powerful columns.'[16] Gorchakov ordered the Odessa

Regiment to thunder on its drums and shout 'Hurrah!', and this succeeded in halting the French until the 2nd Cuirassier Division came up and cleared the neighbourhood of the redoubt. In the darkness one of the infantry regiments of the main French army wandered into the midst of the Russian cuirassiers, and lost five guns and three hundred men before it found its way home.

While Gorchakov was holding firm around the Shevardino Redoubt the flanks of his position were crumbling. The fresh and powerful divisions of Morand and Friant took the village of Shevardino and cleared the jaegers from the nearby woods. Away to the south Major-General Karpov's cossacks reported that the Poles of Poniatowski were working steadily northeast. The redoubt was now clearly untenable, and at midnight Gorchakov received the order to fall back with the grenadiers to the main body of the Second West Army.

According to Labaume the firing had scarcely ended 'when the Russians, whose camp resembled a vast amphitheatre, lighted innumerable fires. The whole of their camp was one vast uninterrupted blaze of light, which, while it presented a grand and sublime appearance, formed a striking contrast with our bivouac, where the soldiers, unable to procure wood, reposed in utter darkness, and heard no sounds but the groans of the wounded.'[17]

As the wind drove a fine rain across the dark and smoking plain, Napoleon heard with astonishment that not a single prisoner had been taken from the enemy. This was a strange and disconcerting fact, and General Caulaincourt ventured the not entirely convincing explanation that the Russians had lost the habit of surrendering because they remembered how all their captured men were invariably killed by the Turks.

In the Russian camp the generals spoke bitterly about the miscalculations which had resulted in 18,000 men being pitted against 35,000 French. Most people would have agreed with General Ermolov that the construction of the Bagration Flèches had made the Shevardino Redoubt superfluous, 'for it stood out of artillery range and consequently there was no point in defending and maintaining it'.[18] Far from screening the left, he said, the defence of the redoubt had brought on an action which permitted the enemy to sound out this vulnerable

8 General M. B. Barclay de Tolly, creator and effective leader of the Russian army at Borodino. (*Novosti Press Agency*)

9 General P. I. Bagration, Commander of the Russian Second West Army at Borodino. He was mortally wounded in the fight for the Bagration Fleches.

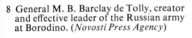

10 Field-Marshal M. I. Kutuzov; focus of Russian loyalties in the campaign of 1812.

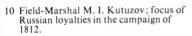

11 General L. L. Bennigsen; the viciously egocentric Russian Chief of Staff at Borodino.

12 General D. S. Dokhturov; Commander
of VI Corps.

13 Major-General A. I. Kutaisov; author of
General Rules for the Artillery, and Commander
of the First West Army. He was killed at Borodino

14 General M. A. Miloradovich; overall
Commander of the Russian right at
Borodino.

15 M. I. Platov; General of Cavalry and Ataman
of the Don Cossacks. (*Novosti Press Agency*)

flank. Barclay was disgusted with the whole affair. He had wanted the redoubt to be abandoned in good time, but the high command insisted that the troops should not be allowed to fall back before they came under direct attack. Barclay explains that 'the reason evidently was that Bennigsen had chosen the position, and he did not want to lose face. Consequently on 5 September he sacrificed six or seven thousand brave soldiers and three guns.'[19] Barclay also pointed out that the Old Smolensk Road was wide open to penetration by a flanking movement, 'yet Prince Kutuzov and Bennigsen asserted that it would be easy enough to defend that road with the *opolchenie*'.[20] In the event the whole of Tuchkov's III Corps had to be moved down to plug the gap (see p. 74).

Such recriminations did not bode very well for the working-together of the generals in the great battle that was looming ahead.

There is an element of drama about the uninterrupted calm which reigned throughout 6 September, the day that separated the action at Shevardino from the tragedy of the 7th. Hardly a shot was exchanged between the rival armies, lying little more than a mile apart. The Russians had no intention of stampeding the French into an attack before their own preparations were complete, while Napoleon needed a little more time to work out his plan of battle and await the arrival of the reserve artillery and Latour-Maubourg's IV Cavalry Corps.

As the sun climbed in a flawless autumn sky Napoleon rode slowly on his horse *L'Embelli* along the whole length of the line of battle. He was suffering from a heavy cold, and his bladder complaint recurred so acutely that he dismounted several times and bowed his head in pain. The Emperor returned to his tent at nine in the morning, rather dissatisfied with what he had been able to see. He mounted again at two in the afternoon and repeated the tour. The thickness of the brushwood and the danger from the Russian jaegers prevented him from getting close enough to see whether there was a gap between the southernmost of the Bagration Flèches and the right wing of Tuchkov's III Corps; the northernmost flèche escaped his view entirely, and he went into battle on the next day under the erroneous impression that his army would have only two fortifications to overcome. Furthermore he mistook

81

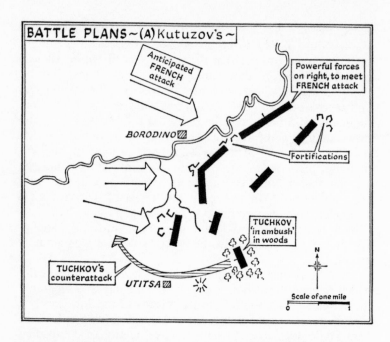

BATTLE PLANS ~ (A) Kutuzov's ~

Anticipated FRENCH attack

Powerful forces on right, to meet FRENCH attack

BORODINO

Fortifications

TUCHKOV 'in ambush' in woods

TUCHKOV'S counterattack

UTITSA

N

Scale of one mile

0   1

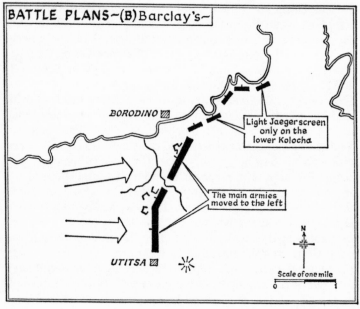

BATTLE PLANS ~ (B) Barclay's ~

BORODINO

Light Jaeger screen only on the lower Kolocha

The main armies moved to the left

UTITSA

N

Scale of one mile

0   1

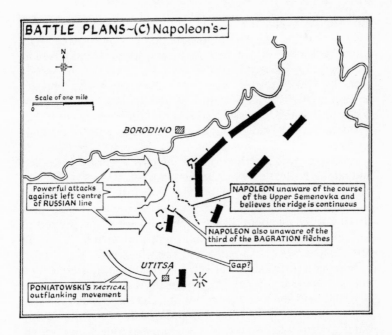

BATTLE PLANS ~(C) Napoleon's~

N

Scale of one mile
0   1

BORODINO

Powerful attacks
against left centre
of RUSSIAN line

NAPOLEON unaware of the course
of the Upper Semenovka and
believes the ridge is continuous

NAPOLEON also unaware of the
third of the BAGRATION flèches

Gap?

UTITSA

PONIATOWSKI'S *TACTICAL*
outflanking movement

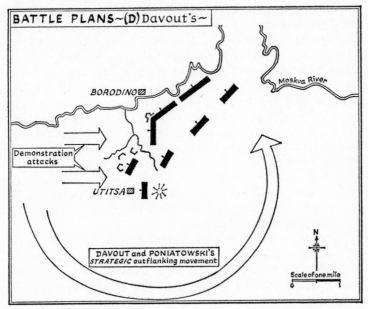

BATTLE PLANS ~(D) Davout's~

BORODINO

Moskva River

Demonstration
attacks

UTITSA

DAVOUT and PONIATOWSKI'S
STRATEGIC outflanking movement

N

Scale of one mile
0   1

the minute Kamenka rivulet for the headwaters of the Semenovka, and failed to appreciate that the upper Semenovka could be traced all the way past Semenovskaya and behind the Bagration Flèches to a source on the fringe of the woods near the Old Smolensk Road (an error which also appears on the earliest French maps of the battle); he therefore assumed that the Raevsky Redoubt and the Bagration Flèches stood on the same ridge, and he planned to assault them simultaneously.

Napoleon was standing on the heights opposite Borodino and taking in the scene for the last time when Marshal Davout hastened up from the right and asked for permission to combine Poniatowski's V Corps and his own I Corps in a striking force of about 40,000 men, with which he wanted to roll up the Russian left flank and rear and thereby finish off 'the Russian army, the battle and the whole war!'[21]

Napoleon listened attentively, meditated for a time and finally pronounced: 'No! The movement is altogether too great. It would lead me away from my objective and make me lose too much time.'[22] Davout was inclined to argue the point, but Napoleon silenced him and the Marshal rode off muttering. Napoleon returned to camp, where Murat told him that the Russians were about to retreat. Napoleon was alarmed at the prospect of the enemy evading him a third time, and he returned forthwith to the heights opposite Borodino, 'from where he could see the long dark columns of troops covering the main road (the New Smolensk Road) and uncoiling in the plain, as well as the long convoys of waggons which were coming up with provisions and ammunition. Everything indicated that the Russians intended to stay put and give battle. Napoleon had only a few officers with him, so as not to draw attention and fire from the enemy, but at that very moment he was recognized in the Russian batteries and a cannon shot broke the silence of that day.'[23] His doubts set at rest, Napoleon returned to camp to dictate the orders for the next day's battle and compose a suitable proclamation.

So it was that the Emperor rejected Davout's suggestion for a strategic outflanking movement, a 'Napoleonic' concept if ever there was one, and preferred to launch an unimaginative frontal attack against prepared positions. Napoleon thereby doomed many thousands of his men before a shot was fired. What was he thinking of? Certainly Davout's move would have deprived the army of a large number of men for a long time, as Napoleon pointed out, and the night march through heavily wooded terrain would have tested the commanders' sense of direction and told heavily on the horses of the cavalry and artillery. Also there was reason to believe that the Russians would decamp if they had suspected any such move. All these arguments are tenable; yet it is difficult to dispel the suspicion that Napoleon may have rejected the more enterprising course because he was already sinking in the lethargy that was to engulf him on the day of the battle. Transpose Gettysburg for Borodino, General Longstreet for Marshal Davout and the year 1863 for 1812, and we arrive at a corresponding stage in the career of the Confederate commander Robert E. Lee. Both Lee and Napoleon were mesmerized by the sight of the ground before them and seemed to be incapable of summoning up the mental energy to worst the enemy by a bold manoeuvre rather than a stand-up battle.

Thus Poniatowsky's V Corps was relegated to a purely tactical outflanking movement along the Old Smolensk Road towards Utitsa. This involved no more than 10,000 troops and fifty guns, in other words under eight per cent of the army's manpower and eleven per cent of its artillery. The main blow was to be delivered against the left wing of the Russian army along a sector of about one and a half miles, stretching from the Bagration Flèches north by Semenovskaya to the Raevsky Redoubt. Here Napoleon assembled 85,000 men, or two-thirds of his army. Reading from south to north this massive striking force consisted of the three divisions of Davout's I Corps, with Murat's cavalry (the three reserve cavalry corps of Nansouty, Montbrun and Latour-Maubourg) drawn up in a great block behind. Then came a huge array which extended more than a mile in depth from Morand's division (nearest the enemy) through the packed ranks of the two corps of Ney and Junot to the Guard Cavalry, the Young Guard and the Old Guard (see Map 8. p. 94).

The area north of the Kolocha was covered by Viceroy Eugène's comparatively thinly-spread IV Corps (the Royal Italian Guard, the divisions of Delzons and Broussier and

Ornano's attached cavalry, as well as Gérard's division of I Corps and Grouchy's reserve cavalry corps). IV Corps was to assist the main attack by clearing Borodino village and delivering the first assault against the Raevsky Redoubt.

On 6 September the beams of the rising sun penetrated the mist above the Russian camp and 'glanced off the death-dealing steel of the bayonets and muskets, and played in dazzling flashes on the brass barrels of the artillery. Everyone made ready for the bloody work of the next day. The Moscow *opolchenie* finished off the breastworks of the batteries, dragged the guns into position and prepared the cartridges. The soldiers were busy cleaning and sharpening their bayonets, and pipeclaying their cross-belts.'[24] The pioneers dismantled as many of the timber houses of the villages as they could, and cut ramps to make it easier for the troops to cross some of the steep little valleys.

Kutuzov had no great schemes to revolve in his head, for he was committed to give battle where he stood. Instead of issuing an eloquent proclamation he simply toured the army to the accompaniment of deep Russian hurrahs, which followed him from one regiment to another. He had a little speech for each regiment, like his words to the Simbirsk Infantry: 'To you is given the task of defending our native soil. Serve loyally and honourably to the last drop of your blood! Each regiment will be committed to the battle, but you will be relieved regularly every two hours. I rely on you, and may God be our help!'[25] In the late afternoon the gorgeously-apparelled popes and archimandrites went the round of the camp, swinging their censers, spraying the regimental colours and the shaven heads of the soldiers with holy water, and holding up the icon of the Black Virgin, which had been rescued during the fighting at Smolensk. The army was seized with a religious fervour which reminded one eyewitness of what he had read about Cromwell's men on the day of battle.[26]

The final orders to the Russian army were short and to the point, being mostly concerned with economy and discipline on the day of battle. Kutuzov considered it necessary 'to remind the corps commanders to keep their reserves intact as long as possible, for the general who retains his reserves is unbeaten'.[27] Likewise Barclay ordered Ermolov to tell the corps commanders of the First West Army that they were to be especially careful 'to restrain their men from banging off with their muskets to no purpose, and to get their gunners to economize as far as possible on their ammunition. A rapid harmless fire may astonish the enemy at the beginning of a battle, but it soon loses its power to impress'.[28] The battalion column was to be the accepted formation throughout the two armies, and the attack with the bayonet the fundamental tactic.

Kutaisov, commander of the First West Army's artillery, was anxious to refute an old doctrine which taught that guns must be preserved from capture regardless of the circumstances: in past battles this notion had encouraged some of the more nervous artillerymen to whisk their guns away from the field almost as soon as the enemy were in sight. Now Kutaisov asked his chiefs 'to remind the companies from me that they are not to make off before the enemy are actually sitting on the guns. Tell the commanders and all the officers that they must stand their ground until the enemy are within the closest possible canister range, which is the only way to ensure that we do not cede a yard of our position. The artillery must be prepared to sacrifice itself. Let the anger of your guns roar out! Fire your last charge of canister at point-blank range! A battery which is captured after this will have inflicted casualties on the enemy which will more than compensate for the loss of the guns'.[29] All the evidence indicates that the Russian gunners took Kutaisov at his word.

So much for the ground, the plans and the tactics. What of the size and quality of the forces which were to meet on the following day? Napoleon commanded some 133,000 men, whom he massed on the battlefield at an average density of 44,000 troops per mile (infantry 86–90,000, cavalry 29,500, artillery and engineers 16,000). This force was opposed by about 125,000 Russians, who were distributed along their overextended front at 36,000 to the mile (infantry about 88,000, cavalry about 24,000, artillery and engineers 14,000).

An adding machine would have given Napoleon the advantage. However the purely numerical superiority of the *Grande Armée* was counterbalanced by other factors. The Emperor's 133,000 men were the survivors of 450,000 troops who had set out on the invasion of Russia, which shows how battered, sickly and depleted the regiments which fought at Borodino already were. The cavalry was in a particularly bad way. So many horses had foundered on the road that Napoleon was left with just 29,425 serviceable beasts, which were distributed among eighty-three regiments. Forty-one of these regiments were composed of foreigners, mostly Germans and Poles; the French cavalry regiments proper numbered forty-three, of which the six regiments of Guard cavalry took no part in the battle. The skinny nags of the artillery dragged to the field 587 assorted guns, of which only about one-tenth could be counted as battery pieces.

The Russian army as a whole was better found than Napoleon's. The cavalry was notably fresh and well-mounted, while the gunners not only owned an outright numerical superiority over the French (640 pieces), but enjoyed the advantage of calibre, a quarter of their guns being battery pieces. Unfortunately the training of some of the Russian units left much to be desired. Fifteen thousand of the total of the infantry was made up of the *opolchenie,* and the regular regiments themselves incorporated another fifteen thousand men who were recruits, and had to learn the trade of war as they went along. Likewise nearly one-third of the Russian cavalry was composed of cossacks (7,000), who were of limited use in a set-piece battle.

The twenty-four-year-old Russian general Prince Eugene of Württemburg chatted realistically about the prospects with his adjutant just before the battle. It seemed to Eugène that people like Barclay and Bagration were a good match for Marshals Ney and Davout, though 'the personality of the mighty Napoleon will always tend to tip the scales in his favour. As for our own troops, they are the equal, battalion for battalion, with the nucleus of the French veteran troops: our men are nearly all proven and experienced soldiers [which was not altogether true] and since Vitebsk and Smolensk even the few newly-raised regiments have fought heroically. The enemy are a motley crowd, and they are kept together not so much by inclination and zeal as by compulsion and a sense of military honour. On the other hand the enemy probably have the more experienced colonels and staff officers, because our own people have been ruined on the drill square: we still have not put everything right, and it is doubtful whether we can do so until the war goes on a little longer. Fortunately the raw material of our cavalry and artillery is incomparably better, and good horses and guns are virtually indestructible.'[30]

In the late afternoon of 6 September Napoleon returned to his tented headquarters, which had been pitched in the plain between Shevardino and the Kolocha. He was in one of his 'Ossianising' moods, and more than ready to act out the romantic part which everyone expected of him. He had a splendid prop in the shape of a newly-arrived portrait of the infant King of Rome, his child by his new Empress, Marie Louise of Austria. He set the picture up outside his tent, invited the Guard and his generals to admire it, and then, when the troops were cheering their appreciation he declaimed: 'Take him away! He is too young to look upon a field of battle.'[31] Much less welcome was the coming of an adjutant from Marshal Marmont, who told him that the French had just been defeated by Wellington at Salamanca.

In immediate preparation for the battle, the French were already building five bridges over the Kolocha above Borodino (see Map 5. p. 70), and throwing up three large batteries from which 120 guns were to open the bombardment the following day. In the evening Napoleon called his marshals and senior generals to him, and sent them away with written orders for their divisional commanders: the instructions did not reach some parts of the army until late at night, and the generals had to decipher the vital words in the dancing light of their camp fires.

Another document, Napoleon's proclamation to the army, was circulated at the same time at the level of the battalion and squadron commanders, who were ordered to read it aloud to their men the next morning. The Emperor had weighed the content of the proclamation very carefully: 'for several days now he had been in the midst of the army, and he had found the troops strangely quiet – the kind of silence you associate with a state of great expectation or tension, like the atmosphere before a storm, or the feeling in a crowd of people who are suddenly plunged into a situation of grave danger.'[32]

He sensed the army's desire to see Moscow, its ambition for pillage, but above all its yearning to return home:

'Soldiers! Here is the battle you have so much desired. The victory now depends on you: we have need of it. Victory will give us abundant supplies, good winter quarters and a prompt return to our native land. Fight as you did at Austerlitz, Friedland, Vitebsk and Smolensk, and posterity will remember with pride your conduct on this great day. May it be said of each one of us: "He fought in that great battle under the walls of Moscow!"'

The men who were supposed to do all the fighting were now snatching what sleep they could on 'that extremely restless night. Our ears were ceaselessly assaulted by the endless and confused noise of moving columns of artillery and cavalry.'[33] The Westphalian captain, von Linsingen, was unable to get any rest at all: 'I could not escape the feeling that something huge and destructive was hanging over all of us. This mood led me to look at my men. There they were, sleeping around me on the cold, hard ground. I knew them all very well . . . and I was aware that many of these brave troops would not survive until to-morrow evening, but would be lying torn and bloody on the field of battle. For a moment it was all too easy to wish that the Russians would simply steal away again during the night, but then I remembered how we had suffered over the last few weeks. Better an horrific end than a horror without end! Our only salvation lay in battle and victory!'[34]

Early in the morning, long before daylight, the troops staggered to their feet, shuffled together in their formations, and marched off under the guidance of staff officers to their battle positions. The Imperial proclamation was read out by the colonels and majors at about five or six in the morning.

Even the veterans caught their breath as dawn revealed the army drawn up in unprecedented size and splendour. The troops had been told to look their best, and as one of the Polish officers glanced over his right shoulder towards the Shevardino Redoubt he caught sight of 'the Old Guard standing in their parade uniforms, with their red plumes and epaulettes showing across the fields like a stripe of blood'.[35]

Napoleon was in desperate need of rest, but it is doubtful whether he had slept any better than his soldiers. From his camp bed he repeatedly asked his staff to let him know the time, or whether there were any signs of the Russians making off. After one such call the aide-de-camp Ségur found him with his head in his hands, meditating on the vanities of glory: 'What is war? It is a barbaric trade, in which everything comes down to being the stronger at a given point.'[36] The Emperor then launched into a long discourse about the inconstancy of fortune, the likelihood of victory and, as always, his fear that the Russians would slip away from him. He sank back once more, but was too strained and chilled to fall asleep.

At three in the morning Napoleon roused himself by drinking some punch and talking to another of his aides, General Rapp: 'To-day we shall be at grips with the notorious Kutuzov. You must remember that he was the man who was commandant of Braunau during the Austerlitz campaign. He stayed three months in the fortress without so much as stirring from his room. He didn't even mount his horse to tour the fortifications.'[37]

Napoleon them summoned Berthier and worked until about five, when an officer came from Ney to announce that the Russians were still in position and that the army was awaiting permission to attack. Napoleon called his officers together and went out through the flap in his pavilion. As the soldiers on either side of the exit presented arms he cried out: 'We have them at last! March on! We are going to break open the gates of Moscow!'[38]

He rode on to his chosen command post, by the Shevardino Redoubt in front of the centre of the Guard. 'After he dismounted they brought him a chair. He turned it around and sat astride, with his arms resting on the back, and raising his telescope he keenly surveyed the scene before him.'[39] As the mist dispersed he remarked to his generals: 'It is a trifle cold, but the sun is bright. It is the sun of Austerlitz!'

As soon as dusk had fallen the Russians saw how 'the French camp blazed up in countless fires for fifteen miles around. The flames were reflected in the sky, suffusing the clouds with a blood-red colour . . . an augury of the blood that was about to be shed on the ground.'[40] The troops had had plenty of rest and many of them spent the hours of darkness huddled in their long grey greatcoats around the camp fires, sometimes breaking into dirge-like song.

Lieutenant Bogdanov of the pioneers was one officer who was unusually busy, for General Raevsky had decided that the redoubt was vulnerable to cavalry and asked the pioneers to do something about it. Raevsky had already dug a chain of bone-breaking 'wolf pits' a hundred paces in front of the battery, but he told Bogdanov 'there is still one very important thing which will have to be seen to; while we are holding out in the battery the enemy could easily sweep around our flank and take the fortification from the rear. We must put some formidable obstacles in their path. Make a careful survey of the position and tell me what we ought to be doing and how we should set about it.'[41]

Bogdanov extended the parapet laterally by two twenty-five-yard-long breastworks, one on either side. Using timber and spikes from dismantled houses, he planted a double palisade around the rear of the battery; the inner palisade rose vertically to a height of eight feet, while the outer one sloped menacingly outwards for six and a half feet. Gaps were left at the two ends of the palisade to permit troops and guns to pass between the palisade and the breastwork.

Raevsky inspected the finished work at half-past four, and after ordering a few additions he turned to the officers and said: 'Now, gentlemen, we may rest in security. When daylight comes Napoleon will espy what seems to be a simple open battery, but his army will come up against a virtual fortress. The approaches are swept by more than two hundred cannon (counting the nearby batteries), the ditch is deep and wide and the glacis is solid.'[42]

Early in the morning Barclay awoke in his quarters in a hamlet near the New Smolensk Road and arrayed himself in all his orders and decorations before placing himself at the head of the First West Army. This ostentation was unusual in a man of unassuming habits. Kutuzov too was up early and went out alone to a height near Gorki. He watched the field by the light of the camp fires and soon his staff officers and some of the generals began to group themselves about him.

Bogdanov remembers that at about five in the morning some of the generals were issuing their last instructions 'when suddenly a flash was seen to our left and a cannon shot rang out; this was followed after a while by a second report and then a third. Ten minutes later a fourth shot boomed forth – this was one of ours, replying to the enemy. It began to get light . . .'[43]

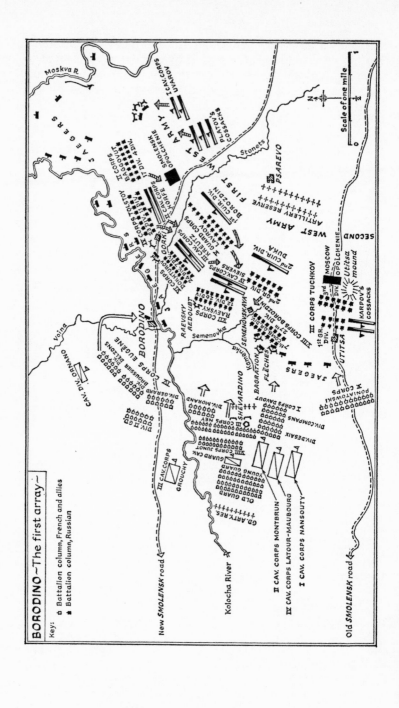

BORODINO ~ The first array ~

Key: ✠ Battalion column, French and allies
        ✠ Battalion column, Russian

Chapter 8

THE BATTLE OF 7 SEPTEMBER

I

The opening bombardment. The first attacks of the Grande Armée.

The French had completed their three enormous batteries during the night, but as daylight began to illuminate the field they discovered that by some inconceivable miscalculation they had built on sites that were out of effective cannon shot of the enemy. They had to drag the guns out and pull them closer. The Russians had a splendid view of the proceedings, for they had the rising sun behind them, but they seemed unwilling to break the terrible silence by disturbing the Frenchmen in their work.

At six o'clock precisely the first shot thundered from a battery of Guard artillery on the right of the French line, and the firing was immediately taken up all along the front of I and III Corps. There was no interval between the shots, and 'the thick clouds of smoke curled from the batteries into the sky and darkened the sun, which seemed to veil itself in a blood-red shroud.'[1]

The Russian artillery took up the challenge. A Russian gunner standing well to the rear of the right flank reports that 'the enemy shot flew towards us in their last bounds, or rolled through the grass with their last impetus. Shells burst in the air and showered splinters with a horrid noise.'[2] One of the roundshot descended through a tent where a Russian artillery colonel was regaling his officers, and landed gently on the man's stomach. The colonel calmly picked up the ball and rolled it among the plates, saying 'Well, my friends, here's something for you to bite on'.[3] Unfortunately he died a few days later from internal injuries.

In the front lines the missiles drove through masses of men and horses, or passed close overhead and produced an

95

involuntary shudder in the ranks from the pressure of the air. That was why 'veteran soldiers, who awaited the bursting of a shell with equanimity, would duck or move whenever a shot flew near them.'[4] Colonel Seruzier of the French artillery experienced another odd effect of gunfire when a shell exploded in his horse's stomach, launching him in a spectacular somersault and depositing him safely on the ground. The same thing was seen to happen to a Russian cavalryman. For hours on end the intensity of the gunfire hardly abated, and the ground around the Raevsky Redoubt eventually looked 'like a stormy sea. The earth had been pulverized by the coming and going of the troops, and with every canister ball flogging up a little cloud of dust the whole area crawled like moving waves.'[5]

The first Russian unit to feel the impact of the French attack was the Lifeguard Jaeger Regiment, which was marooned beyond the Kolocha in the village of Borodino. Barclay believed that it would have been enough to station an observation post in Borodino, and he was angry at General Ermolov for having persuaded Kutuzov and Bennigsen to put a whole regiment at risk in this isolated position. His fears were confirmed when he received a report at daybreak from Colonel Bistrom, commander of the Lifeguard Jaegers, that he had seen some movement in the French positions. Barclay sent General Löwenstern to order the jaegers to pull out of the village and burn the bridge over the river, but Löwenstern had hardly arrived before the mist dispersed and columns of French infantry were seen to be marching to the attack 'with unbelievable speed'.[6]

The assault on Borodino had been launched by Delzons' division of Prince Eugène's IV Corps. The French caught the jaegers completely off their guard, and while one of the columns bundled the Russians out of the village at bayonet point, the other threw out a chain of skirmishers along the Kolocha and opened fire just as the enemy were crowding on to the bridge. 'We were so cramped,' wrote Löwenstern, 'that every French musket ball found its mark.'[7] In these fifteen minutes the Lifeguard Jaegers lost thirty officers and something like half their men.

There was no time to destroy the bridge, and the surviving

96

16 Lieutenant-General F. P. Uvarov,
wearing a white cuirassier's uniform.

17 Lieutenant-General A. P. Ermolov; Chief of
Staff of the First West Army; mainly remem-
bered for his part in wresting the Raevsky
Redoubt back from Morand's Division.

19 Lieutenant-General N. N. Raevsky; Commander
of VI Corps; chiefly responsible for the building
and defence of the redoubt which bore his name.

18 Lieutenant-General D. P. Neverovsky;
Commander of the 27th Division.

20 View from the site of the Raevsky Redoubt, showing the field of fire
northwards to Borodino church, which is seen in the centre of the photograph.
The Russian VI Corps held the ground on the right-hand side. Just discernible
on the left is the top of a Russian pillbox of 1941. *(photo: David Chandler)*

21 Reconstruction of guns at the Raevsky Redoubt. *(photo: Michaeljohn Harris)*

jaegers streamed up the slope on the far side of the Kolocha, hotly pursued by the 106th Regiment of the Line. However the panting Frenchmen rapidly got out of order, and General Plauzonne was shot dead as he was hastening across the bridge to call them back. At this juncture the 106th was hit in the right flank by the 1st Russian Jaeger Regiment and the remnants of the Lifeguard Jaegers, who had been rallied by Colonel Vuich. Pursued by musketry and canister the 106th fell back into the arms of its comrades of the 92nd Regiment, which had crossed the Kolocha in support, and both regiments beat a retreat over the bridge.

The Russians re-occupied most of the lost ground, but Barclay had no wish to re-stage a fight which had cost him 'one of the best regiments of the Lifeguard to no purpose whatsoever.'[8] The jaegers were accordingly ordered to fall back to the main position, and this time they took good care to burn the bridge to its foundations. The French moved forward again, and Eugène planted twenty-eight pieces near Borodino so as to bring the Russian batteries at Gorki and the northern flank of the Raevsky Redoubt under fire. Eugène had little further use for the village itself, and seeing that the Russians had lost interest in it he pulled back two divisions to his main line of battle, leaving just Delzons' division and a force of cavalry to hold the village and the left bank of the Kolocha.

As soon as the crisis at Borodino bridge was over, Barclay began to ride south through his First West Army. For the moment there seemed to be no French assault in the offing for this part of the line, though the shot and shell were ploughing up the earth all about him. In the course of the tour he passed in front of the Preobrazhensky and Semenovsky Lifeguard regiments, where 'the young grenadiers preserved a truly military bearing and calmly welcomed his appearance. The shots were already working to devastating effect in their midst, but the men stood just as stoically and silently as before, with their muskets by their sides, and they coolly closed up their ranks whenever a missile claimed its victims.'[9] However, the strain proved too great for General Lavrov, the commander of V Corps, who was reduced by the bombardment to a state of total mental and physical collapse.

Meanwhile a murderous battle at close quarters had broken out along the left flank of Bagration's Second West Army. By about half past six Napoleon could hear that the fight at Borodino village was in full swing, and judging that Poniatowski must by now have begun his outflanking movement along the Old Smolensk Road, he launched the best part of I Corps in an attack on the southernmost of the Bagration Flèches.

General Compans, the hero of Shevardino, was given the honour of leading the advance. He formed his men into two groups: the one on the right was supposed to clear the Russian jaegers from the woods to the south, while the group on the left was directed straight at the fortification. The division of General Desaix followed up behind. The attack was supported by 102 guns, and 'suddenly the peaceful plain and the silent hills erupted in swirls of fire and smoke, followed almost at once by countless explosions, and the howling of canon shot that ripped through the air in every direction.'[10] 'Soon the heads of the columns of troops disappeared into a cloud of dust which the radiant sun . . . impregnated with a reddish glow. The deafening din of our cannonade was interspersed with a sound that seemed like a distant echo, and came from the batteries on the left around Borodino, and on the right, beyond the woods, where Prince Poniatowski was engaged in combat.'[11]

The French marched into a storm of canister fire from the Russian 11th and 32nd Artillery Companies, which were sited in front of the flèches. A Russian gunner general records that 'the execution wrought by our batteries was frightful, and the enemy columns faded away perceptibly despite the continual reinforcements which arrived. The more effort the enemy put into the attack the more their casualties were piled up.'[12]

The French also came under fire from General Shakhovsk's jaegers who were swarming in the brushwood, and at half past seven Compans was put out of action by a musket shot in the right shoulder. Davout's horse was shot dead shortly after, and the marshal was so shocked and bruised by the fall that he had to be carried from the field. Though General Desaix galloped up to take command, nobody seems to have been interested in putting Compans' plan for the two-pronged attack into effect. The 57th Regiment actually seized the southernmost fortification and occupied it for a short time, but the Russian jaegers kept up their peppering from the woods and before long the depleted French were driven back by the 7th Combined Grenadier Division, which formed the garrison proper. According to General Ermolov 'it was only the superiority of that weapon [the bayonet] in the hands of the Russian soldiers that enabled us to maintain our resistance so long.'[13] He should also have mentioned that the French were already badly shot-up, and that the Russian engineers had deliberately left the Bagration Flèches open at the rear to facilitate counter-attacks of this kind. General Sievers now brought up the New Russian Dragoons, the Litovsk Lancers and the Akhtyrka Hussars, and followed up the victory by chasing the French some way towards their main positions.

The French must have been repulsed from the Bagration Flèches at about the same time as Prince Poniatowski began his private war for the Utitsa area. Kutuzov explains that the ground was of such great importance 'because the hill there commanded the whole neighbourhood, and if the enemy seized it they would have been able to take our left wing in the flank and made it impossible for us to hold out on the Old Smolensk Road.'[14]

Poniatowski's Poles had got under way at daybreak, but they moved so slowly that it was not until about eight o'clock that they began to exchange shots with the first Russian troops in their path. These belonged to Lieutenant-General P. A. Stroganov's 1st Grenadier Division, deployed in two lines to act as a kind of screen to the main body of Tuchkov's III Corps, which was grouped in battalion columns behind. The Russians stood in dangerously open ground, thanks to Bennigsen's intervention on the day before (see p. 74). Moreover, Tuchkov had been forced to weaken his Corps by sending Konovnitsyn with the four regiments of the 3rd Division to help out in the defence of the Bagration Flèches. After a short but costly battle Tuchkov therefore ordered the first line of grenadiers to set fire to Utitsa village and fall back on the second line. Poniatowski duly occupied the ground and halted to lick his wounds.

During the ensuing lull the balance swung still further in

99

favour of the Poles. Part of Junot's VIII Corps came down, at Napoleon's command, to evict the Russian jaegers from the wood between the Utitsa area and the Bagration Flèches. Moreover Tuchkov, already hard-pressed, had to detach a number of his dragoons to help the Second West Army around the Bagration Flèches, which reduced the strength of III Corps to four thousand men and thirty-six guns.

Poniatowski came to life again at half-past ten, and his gunners prepared the way for a new push by bringing twenty-two pieces to bear agains the Utitsa mound.

The whole Russian army would have stood in grave danger if Poniatowski had been allowed to continue his fitful advances. Kutuzov, Barclay and Colonel Toll all seem to have awakened to this emergency at the same time, and a rapid summons was sent to Lieutenant-General Baggovut, the commander of II Corps, one of the units uselessly strung out along the Kolocha on the far right of the Russian position.

At first Baggovut was told to send his 17th Division to the left; then came the order to detach the 4th Division as well, and soon all II Corps except its six jaeger regiments was streaming southwards behind the main army. ' "How are things going over there?" asked Baggovut of one of the staff officers. "They could hardly be worse," was the reply. "We are finished if you don't hurry up. Bagration's army has been pounded into the ground, and it's a miracle that Tuchkov is still hanging on." '[15]

Baggovut's troops were delighted to be going into action at last, and the pace began to quicken of its own accord. 'More and more cannon shot crashed into the undergrowth to right and left and showered our heads with branches. Straight in front of us a ball landed in the Minsk Regiment, which formed the head of our column; immediately afterwards came a second and then a third. Soon we lost all count of the casualties.'[16] II Corps was soon marching through some of the hottest fighting of the day in the central sector of the battlefield, and Baggovut had to leave two regiments of the 17th Division behind to help remedy the situation while he continued on his way with the 4th Division. As a further good deed Baggovut dropped off some pieces of the 17th Artillery Company to help the badly-outgunned horse artillery of IV Corps, and then, at Tuchkov's urgent request, he sent ahead the Belozersk and Willmanstrand infantry regiments and six battery pieces of the 17th Company under command of Colonel Glukhov.

Tuchkov directed Glukhov's guns on to the Utitsa mound just in time for them to be greeted by Poniatowski's twenty-two-gun battery. For a while Glukhov duelled valiantly with the enemy artillery, but the Polish columns were closing in so fast that he had to limber up and abandon the hill. Fortunately the reinforcements from II Corps were now at hand. The Belozersk Regiment beat off a final attack on the part of the Poles, and then at about noon II Corps and the remnants of III Corps moved forward, sweeping the enemy from the hill and as far as Utitsa village. The stouthearted Tuchkov was mortally wounded in the head of the Pavlov Grenadiers, and the command of this remote but bitterly-contested part of the battlefield passed to General Baggovut.

II

The Battle for the Bagration Flèches.

We left Davout's I Corps recovering its strength after the repulse of its first attack on the Bagration Flèches. Compans' 5th Division had taken the brunt of the fighting, and the troops were now scattered in ditches and folds in the ground while the commanders planned the next attack. General Girod de l'Ain describes how the 5th Division's temporary commander, Desaix, stood in the open 'examining the positions and movements of the Russian troops we had before us. I was with him, taking in the same view, when a bullet hit one of his saddle holsters, smashing a bottle of brandy which he had taken good care to bring with him. He was stricken to the heart, but he turned to me with the good-humoured remark: "It's the fault of your rotten white horse for drawing their fire." '[1]

At that moment General Rapp came from Napoleon with orders to take over the 5th Division, so setting Desaix free to resume command of the 4th division which now replaced the battered 5th in the front line. This time Ney's III Corps was involved in the fighting through the participation of the four

101

regiments of Ledru's division, which was given the responsibility of reducing what seemed to the French to be the
northernmost of the Bagration Flèches – they still did not
know that the Russians had a *third* fortification in their right
rear – while to their right Junot's VIII Corps was making
ready to rout the Russian jaegers from the woods which lay
along the southern flank of the open ground in front of the
Bagration Flèches.

The Russians were feeding more troops into that area.
Tuchkov, who was not yet under pressure, sent thither General
Konovnitsyn with the 3rd Division (Regiments Chernigov,
Muromsk, Revel and Selinginsk). Help was also on the way
from the centre and right, despite a turmoil of orders, counter-
orders and misunderstandings. Kutuzov was the first to break
his own rule about not draining the reserve, and did not
hesitate to order Grand Duke Constantine to send off the
three Lifeguard Cavalry regiments of 1st Cuirassier Division,
as well as eight compound grenadier battalions, the Lifeguard
Horse Artillery and two companies of the Lifeguard Foot
Artillery; Barclay also did his bit by dispatching II Corps on
its long march from the extreme right.

The French, however, got their new attack under way before
the Russian reinforcements could intervene, and so the immediate task of holding the Bagration Flèches fell once more
upon the 7th Combined Grenadier Division. In the words of
that gallant unit's commander, General Vorontsov, 'an hour
later it ceased to exist'.[2]

Desaix's troops led the assault. They had moved only a
short distance before a tempest of Russian cuirassiers charged
past the heads of the columns and flooded over a thirty-gun
battery to the left. The Russian horse was driven back by a
spirited counter-attack but the infantry had scarcely resumed
the advance when it came under several destructive volleys of
canister from a battery which had crept up behind the cuirassiers. General Rapp was in the forefront of the battle. He was
twice bruised by spent musket balls, and a third bullet ripped
through his left sleeve and grazed his arm. Rapp prided himself
on his collection of battle wounds, but even he must have
felt he had had enough when a fourth shot caught him in the
left hip and threw him from his horse. General Desaix took

over the command of both divisions, only to be incapacitated almost at once by a musket ball which shattered his left forearm.

One can only suppose that the greater part of the storm of canister and bullets passed over the heads of the rank and file of the French infantry. At any rate enough men survived in the four regiments of Ledru's division to swamp the central and southern Bagration fortifications and wipe out the last of Vorontsov's grenadiers. Only now did the French see that the enemy were holding a third fortification, which lay to the north, and they did not have long to digest the unpleasant discovery before Bagration came at them with six infantry regiments and General Duka's five regiments of cuirassiers – all fresh and eager troops.

The French recoiled from the fortifications, but Murat was now taking a personal hand in affairs and he organized a counter-attack by the 1st Württemburg Jaeger Battalion and the 72nd French Infantry Regiment which won the southern-most flèche a second time. This in turn provoked a charge of the Russian cuirassiers, and in the subsequent confusion Murat had to hop into the fortification and seek refuge with the Württemberg jaegers. He took off his plumed hat, so as to make himself less conspicuous, and 'knowing little or no German he cried out: *Ah, brav Jäger, brav Jäger, scheuss, scheuss, Jäger!* He meant to encourage the troops but the effect was merely comical.'[3] The jaegers understood what Murat meant, even though his *scheuss* bore an unfortunate resemblance to another German word, and they fired away with a will until the rest of the Württemburgers came to the rescue.

The second French attack involved two or more hours of confused fighting in which some historians claim to be able to distinguish four separate pushes. All we know for certain is that the flèches changed hands several times more, and that the French finally committed something like 45,000 men to the struggle. The Russian defence was aggressive in the extreme, and one of their officers writes that 'all our columns of the left flank advanced with the bayonet, and a bloody hand-to-hand combat was the result . . . Cavalry, infantry and gunners, all were thrown together in the heat of battle, and they struck out with bayonets, musket butts, swords and rammers, trampling the fallen underfoot.'[4] To the French it seemed that the Russian formations 'came on at the command of their chiefs like moving fortresses that gave out flashes of steel and bursts of flame. In the open ground they were shot up by our canister and came under alternating attack from our cavalry and infantry, yet despite their huge losses these valiant warriors would draw their last forces together and come against us as before.'[5]

The real murderer was undoubtedly the artillery, for the French managed to assemble no less than four hundred guns on this sector against three hundred pieces of the Russians. According to one of the Russians 'the shells burst in the air as well as on the ground, while the solid shot came buzzing from every side, ploughing the ground with their ricochets and smashing into splinters every object they encountered in their flight. The cannonade . . . was incessant, and the sound was like a continuous peal of thunder.'[6] The performance of the French themselves was magnificent. They pressed home their attacks under murderous canister fire, and in recognition of their bravery the chivalrous Bagration 'several times clapped his hands and shouted *"bravo! bravo!"* '[7]

It must have been some time before ten o'clock when a bullet struck Bagration in the leg and lodged in the bone. He tried to conceal what had happened to him, but he swayed and fell from his horse in sight of hundreds of his men. A mistaken report of his death spread rapidly through the Second West Army, causing almost total demoralization. Bagration unwillingly agreed to be carried away, and as a party of soldiers bore him to the rear he repeatedly turned his head to see what he could of the course of the battle. He was finally deposited on the grass and left to the ministrations of the surgeons, who tried to extract the ball from the leg. Bagration saw Löwenstern approaching from the direction of the First West Army, and, despite the agonizing probings, managed to say: 'Tell General Barclay that the fate and salvation of the army depends on him. So far everything has been going well, but now Barclay ought to come to my army in person.'[8]

Barclay was thunderstruck when the news was brought to him, but since the enemy were already manoeuvring to attack

1. The Central Bagration Fleche. The salient of the V-shaped fortification lies to the left. The embrasures in the right-hand branch show up clearly. (*David Chandler*)

2. The Kolocha Stream below Borodino (*David Chandler*)

3. The 'Nice Byzantine Church' at Borodino (*David Chandler*)

4.   French Troops advancing

5.   French Guns Firing

6. Russian troops moving up

7. After the Battle

his own front he could do little to bolster up Bagration's army except move Ostermann-Tolstoy's IV Corps south to plug the line between the left flank of Raevsky's VII Corps and the right wing of the Lifeguard Infantry Division, which had already been brought from the reserve into the front line. The command of the orphaned Second West Army devolved first upon Konovnitsyn, who ran about in his nightcap frantically trying to restore some kind of order, and then upon General Dokhturov, a more phlegmatic man. The arrival of Tolstoy's corps helped to shore up Raevsky's command and the Lifeguards north of Semenovskaya (as we shall see in a later section), but further south the survivors of Borozdin's VIII Corps were already driven from the flèches and scattered into small groups. Konovnitsyn and Dokhturov accordingly gave up the battle for this bloodstained stretch of ground and withdrew their troops behind the little valley of the Semenovka.

Thus after a battle of about five hours the French had finally beaten the Russians from the Bagration Flèches. By now, however, we have run ahead of our story, and it is time to see how the French were faring in their attacks against the major strongpoint of the Russian right centre, the Raevsky Redoubt.

III

The first attacks on the Raevsky Redoubt.

On the left wing of the *Grande Armée* Prince Eugène spent the early morning re-arranging his troops after the capture of Borodino. He stationed Delzons' division in the village itself, and brought the divisions of Morand, Gérard and Broussier across the pontoon bridges which had been thrown over the Kolocha above the village (see p. 89). By half past nine he was ready to launch an attack up the gently sloping ground against the Raevsky Redoubt.

Eugène's very slowness proved pernicious to the defenders of this sector of the Russian line, for the left wing of the Second West Army was already in desperate trouble and the Russian high command began to think of its right wing as a disposable reserve. Raevsky's overstretched VII Corps was supposed to defend the Redoubt proper as well as a long stretch of ground to the south, in the direction of Semenovskaya. The corps was already down to sixteen battalions before the battle began, for two regiments were away recruiting in the interior of Russia, and two more had been detached with Konovnitsyn to reinforce Tuchkov at Utitsa. Raevsky had been warned by Barclay that he might well be called upon to yield still further troops, and sure enough the whole of VII Corps' second line was taken from him as soon as the combat began. A solitary but welcome accession of strength was General Vuich's 19th Jaeger Regiment, which Raevsky positioned in the ravine behind the redoubt. The remaining eight battalions were too feeble to defend the ground in a continuous line, so Raevsky arrayed them in a counter-attack formation of battalion columns in the same ravine as the jaegers: General Vasil'chikov's 12th Division (four line battalions) took up station on the left, and General Paskevich's 26th Division (four line battalions) on the right.

The redoubt itself was too cramped to hold any infantry, so Schulmann's 26th Artillery Brigade was expected to defend the parapet as well as serve the eighteen heavy guns. Raevsky was also there. A few days earlier he had impaled himself on a bayonet projecting from a cart, and the wounded leg was so painful that he decided to station himself in the redoubt, from where he could see all his corps without moving. He told Schulmann to defend the guns to the last, though he added that the gunners should send the draught horses and ammunition carts away if there seemed to be a real danger of the enemy breaking in. This would prevent the French from turning the guns against the Russians or hauling them away.

Eugène prepared the way for his attack with a violent bombardment. The Russian III Cavalry Corps was standing to the left rear of the redoubt, and suffered particularly from French gunfire. One company of its horse artillery was annihilated, and a second, which came up to replace it, was also wiped out: 'the horses and men were struck down, the ammunition boxes blown up and the guns wrecked'.[1]

Towards ten o'clock Broussier's division made a reconnaissance in force. The French were thrown back easily enough, but they left Raevsky in no doubt that they had something much more serious in store for him. Shortly afterwards General Konovnitsyn sent word that Bagration had been wounded, and asked him to leave the redoubt and go to Semenovskaya. Raevsky replied that he could not budge, and told Konovnitsyn that he would have to muddle through as best he could. Raevsky wrote afterwards that 'this was a really decisive moment, and I could not have abandoned my own post under any kind of pretence. My guns began to thunder out when the enemy came within range, and the smoke hid the French so completely that we could see nothing of their array or ascertain what progress they were making. There was one of my orderly officers standing a little to the left of me, and after a second volley he cried out: "Your Excellency, save yourself!" I turned around and fifteen yards away I saw that French grenadiers were pouring into my redoubt with fixed bayonets.'[2]

This second attack was put in by Morand's division, which advanced in the mixed formation of column and line called 'linked brigades'. The 30th Regiment of the Line was directed straight at the redoubt and one of its officers remembers that 'entire files and half-platoons fell under the enemy fire, leaving great gaps. General Bonamy, who was at the head of the 30th, made us halt in the thickest of the canister fire, and after he rallied us we went forward again at the *pas de charge*. A line of Russian troops [probably jaegers] tried to halt us, but we delivered a regimental volley at thirty paces and passed over the wreckage. We then threw ourselves on the redoubt and climbed in by the embrasures; I myself entered an embrasure the moment after its cannon had fired. The Russian gunners tried to beat us back with traversing-spikes and rammers, and we found them truly formidable adversaries as we grappled with them hand-to-hand. At the same time a large number of French soldiers fell into the wolf-pits and landed on Russian troops who had already tumbled in. Once inside the redoubt I fought the Russian gunners with my sword, and in the process I cut down more than one of them.'[3] The impetus of the 30th Regiment carried it fifty yards beyond the redoubt, but except for a battalion of the 13th Light Infantry the rest of Morand's division was too heavily engaged outside the redoubt to think of exploiting the gap. Raevsky hobbled out of the redoubt during the confusion, and was forced to watch the rest of the fight as an impotent spectator.

Barclay had been riding south from Gorki when he first noticed the commotion at the Raevsky Redoubt. The smoke and flame prevented him from seeing what exactly was taking place, and he sent General Löwenstern ahead to investigate. Löwenstern discovered that the redoubt was in the hands of the French and that the jaegers had dissolved. He sent an officer to tell Barclay what had happened and rode on his white horse to the wing of the unengaged VI Corps and made a theatrical summons to a battalion of the Tomsk Regiment to follow him to the hill.

The First West Army's Chief-of-Staff happened to be passing behind the redoubt at the same time. Ermolov had been sent by Kutuzov to restore the troops on the left to order after Bagration's wound, but he soon appreciated that he had still more urgent business to attend to at the Redoubt. In his own words, 'in many places our jaegers were not only fleeing in disorder but were putting up no resistance at all. The 18th, 19th and 40th Jaegers were in complete panic and disarray, and they were giving the enemy an opportunity to consolidate their gains.'[4] Ermolov caught hold of the third battalion of the Ufimsk Regiment (from Likhachev's division) and advanced on the hill, sweeping up the jaegers on the way. Meanwhile Generals Vasil'chikov and Paskevich had rallied the 12th and 26th Divisions and were moving to pinch out the French salient from either flank.

Bonamy was therefore assailed from four directions at once. Wolzogen writes that 'the attack was executed in astonishingly good order. The various columns approached the foot of the hill in an even step to the time of the drum, and not a single cry arose from the troops. All of this so intimidated the French that we could clearly see that many men were fleeing from the ranks and that the garrison of the redoubt was diminishing perceptibly. The French kept up a fire on the advancing columns only from their cannon, which they had not managed to bring forward in any great quantity. Our troops reached the hill, and then to a general hurrah they carried the summit and the fortification.'[5]

The fighting lasted less than ten minutes. The jaegers were

out for revenge, and 'so as to encourage the troops still further Ermolov took out some crosses of the Order of St George, which he happened to have in his pocket, and threw them in the direction of the redoubt.'[6] The 30th Regiment was pushed through the embrasures at bayonet point, and suffered further heavy losses outside at the hands of 'dead' Russian soldiers who suddenly came to life – the spiritual ancestors of the 'resurrection men' the British were to meet in the Crimea.

The 30th made an attempt to re-form and mount a new attack, but it was again left unsupported by the rest of its division and the 268 survivors had to fall back through the brushwood. Barclay estimated that 'this episode cost the French no less than three thousand casualties, for the hill and the ground about were strewn with enemy corpses for a distance of several hundred yards.'[7]

General Bonamy was immobilized by fifteen wounds, and to save himself from being skewered by a Russian grenadier he cried out that he was Murat, King of Naples. The grenadier seized him by the collar and dragged him proudly off to the generalissimo. He was brought to Kutuzov 'in a frightfully battered state and reeling from side to side, whether from wounds or other causes. "Doctor!" was Kutuzov's cry on seeing him, and after exchanging a few words with the wounded man he had him carried away. Under the uniform of the French hero were found two undershirts, and beneath them again his whole body was ripped with wounds.'[8]

The Russians suffered a severe loss in young General Kutaisov, who forgot his responsibilities as artillery commander and led a party of infantry on an expedition to the right of the Redoubt. He was not seen again, but 'soon his horse galloped past and the bloodstained saddle gave us reason to suppose he had been killed'.[9] There was no one left to supervise the conduct of the artillery, and the movement of guns from the reserve stopped altogether.

The moments that followed the recovery of the Redoubt were the quietest of the battle on this sector of the front. The French artillery fell silent for fear of hitting their own men, who were streaming back from the hill, while the Russians were searching for implements with which to load the abandoned guns in the redoubt. After a few minutes the French began to bring powerful columns forward for a new attack on VII Corps, and, as had happened around the Bagration Flèches, the fighting was a bloody confusion in which it is nearly impossible to distinguish the detail or the sequence of events.

The new attack caught Prince Eugene of Württemburg and the 17th Division of II Corps while they were making their way south to the fighting round Utitsa (see p. 100). The Prince called a halt behind the Redoubt some time after ten o'clock, just when the fortification was being wrested back from the French, and while he was still trying to find out what was going on 'a cloud of dust swept down on us from the left like an avalanche, and the closer it rolled the more monstrous its dimensions appeared.

' "Battalions form squares!" Almost as soon as the command rang out the French cuirassiers came clattering up, while from the other direction the Generals Barclay, Miloradovich and Raevsky threw themselves into our squares, hotly pursued by several regiments of *chasseurs à cheval* and lancers.

'We were completely surrounded, and each of our squares was left to work its own salvation like some warship driven before a storm. The yell of *"En avant!"* rang in our ears, and the force of the onslaught of these mighty masses almost took our breath away.

' "Children!" called the Prince to the soldiers of the Kremenchug Regiment, "take your time, take good aim and look the enemy in the eye!" The troops obeyed willingly. Soon enough the French cavalry emerged from the dust with a gleam of armour, a rattling of their scabbards, and a flashing of the sun on the metal of those helmets of theirs with the horsetail switches. Drunk with victory, this majestic, heroic horde of cavalry pressed home its attack against our iron wall. Only now, when they had taken calm stock of the enemy, did the infantry open fire and surround themselves in a sea of smoke and flame. While the leading cavalrymen crashed to the ground the rearward ranks pushed on, only to fall to fresh salvoes.'[10]

After this hot reception Grouchy's cavalry corps disappeared from view, but the 17th Division soon found itself as hotly engaged as ever. Two regiments of its second brigade lost three hundred men in ten minutes, even though the Russian

III Cavalry Corps (Kreutz) was now at hand to lend some help. Ermolov twice had to turn his guns about to bring them to bear against the enemy at the rear of VII Corps, and the artillerymen were so depleted that they had to be relieved by infantry from the Ufimsk Regiment.

At about eleven o'clock the efforts of the French infantry and cavalry slackened. In compensation the guns suddenly intensified their fire, and it seemed to Barclay 'that Napoleon had decided to annihilate us with his artillery'.[11] Prince Eugene of Württemburg had a horse shot under him. He mounted another which was almost immediately killed in its turn, throwing him to the ground among two writhing officers and a screaming grenadier whose face had been shot away by a cannon ball. An adjutant brought another horse, but Eugene had hardly put his foot in the stirrup when an exploding shell smashed the horse and the officer at the same time. The strong-nerved prince finally acquired an artillery horse and led his second brigade to the area behind the Bagration Flèches, where he arrived at about noon.

Barclay's own suite came under terrible fire. The young adjutant Klinger lost a leg, and Wolzogen had a lucky escape when a cannonball ploughed through his horse and carried away part of his sash. Even the irrepressible Ermolov was rendered hors-de-combat by a canister shot in the neck, and he had to turn the Raevsky Battery over to old Major-General Likhachev, the commander of the 24th Division.

Despite every effort of the left wing of the *Grande Armée* the Russians were still in control of the Raevsky Redoubt, and it was clear that the battle for this important strongpoint was going to be prolonged well into the afternoon.

IV

The fall of Semenovskaya and the crisis of the Russian centre.

While the battles around the Bagration Flèches and the Raevsky Redoubt were raging, Napoleon attacked the left centre of the Russian line. The forces committed to this assault consisted of elements of I Corps (Davout) and III Corps (Ney), as well as a powerful artillery and the two reserve cavalry corps of Nansouty and Latour-Maubourg.

The Russian front around Semenovskaya was an improvised one, composed of forces which had been shifted from other parts of the field. The eight battalions of the 2nd Combined Grenadier Division were stationed immediately in front of the ruined village. They came from the reserve, as did the three magnificent regiments of the Izmail, Litovsk and Finland-Jaeger Lifeguards, which took up post just to the south. Behind the grenadiers and the guardsmen was arrayed the 1st Cuirassier Division. Konovnitsyn and his 3rd Division helped to provide the semblance of a second line of infantry, though they were also concerned in the defence of the Bagration Flèches.

It was about seven in the morning when the French began to manoeuvre themselves into position for the attack. Friant's division of I Corps was aligned directly on the village, while powerful forces of cavalry massed on either flank – Latour-Maubourg's corps to the north, and Nansouty's to the south. As usual the attack was ushered in by a murderous artillery duel, and 'the shot rained down on what was left of Semenovskaya, knocking down the walls and causing the huts to collapse like theatrical scenery. The roaring in the air was continuous and the earth trembled.'[1]

The Saxon lieutenant von Meerheim was in Lorge's division of Saxon and Westphalian cuirassiers, which made up part of Latour-Maubourg's corps, and he writes that as the cavalry trotted forward over the low ridges 'the first cannon shot began to fall in our ranks. It was some compensation that the whole extent of the battle in the central sector was revealed to our eyes, though everything was shrouded in a dense cloud of smoke and all we could make out were the thick masses of our troops, who were swaying backwards and forwards in front of the enemy-held ridge.'[2]

After an agonizing wait under the canister fire Murat's cavalry moved forward at about ten o'clock to cross the Semenovka stream and climb the bank on the far side. Latour-Maubourg's corps came on in columns of half squadrons, and Meerheim remembers that 'the slope was so steep that some riders, who did not appreciate the advantage of climbing obliquely, tumbled over backwards and were trampled by the horses behind. On the top of the hill, about sixty yards from

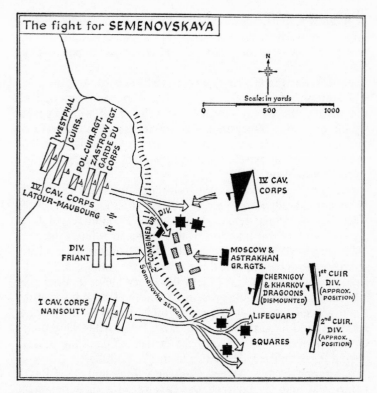

The fight for SEMENOVSKAYA

Scale: in yards
0   500   1000

WESTPHAL CUIRS.
POL. CUIR. RGT.
ZASTROW RGT.
GARDE DU CORPS
IV CAV. CORPS LATOUR-MAUBOURG
DIV. FRIANT
I CAV. CORPS NANSOUTY

2nd COMBINED GR. DIV.
Semenovka stream

IV CAV. CORPS
MOSCOW & ASTRAKHAN GR. RGTS.
CHERNIGOV & KHARKOV DRAGOONS (DISMOUNTED)
1st CUIR DIV. (APPROX. POSITION)
LIFEGUARD SQUARES
2nd CUIR. DIV. (APPROX. POSITION)

the edge, we saw the burnt-out village of Semenovskaya, whose site was marked only by glowing logs.'[3]

The onslaught of the cavalry caught the 2nd Combined Grenadier Division just as it was trying to form itself into three squares. Latour-Maubourg's Germans rode over one of the blocks of swaying grenadiers, then charged between the other two squares without bothering to re-form. Volleys of musketry lashed them from every direction, and many horses and men came to grief when they fell into the underground grain silos which were hidden by the smouldering embers of the village.

Latour-Maubourg's cavalrymen blundered on to the plateau to the north and rear of Semenovskaya, where they promptly came under counter-attack from the Russian IV Cavalry Corps under Major-General Sievers. The Akhtyrka Hussars

113

intervened to particularly deadly effect, for they had somehow armed themselves with lances, and in the desperate mêlée in the trampled-down rye they cut off and destroyed a body of the Saxon cavalry.

Now it was the Russians who were blown and out of order. Thielemann and his officers took the opportunity to call off the rest of the Saxon cavalry and rally them with repeated shouts of 'Halt!' The Russian commanders were trying to do the same with their own men when the compact masses of the Westphalian Cuirassier Brigade appeared on the scene and swept them from the field.

South of Semenovskaya the cuirassiers and light cavalry of Nansouty fared rather worse. Their opponents were the superbly-disciplined Izmail, Litovsk and Finland-Jaeger Lifeguards, who lost no time in forming themselves into impenetrable squares. Whenever the cavalry came surging up the Lifeguardsmen delivered crashing battalion volleys, and 'the French were so near that practically every bullet toppled over a horseman. The terrible cross-fire from the lateral faces of the squares sped thousands of men to their deaths [a slight exaggeration] and filled the rest with terror.'[4] So writes the grateful General Konovnitsyn, who sought shelter in one of the squares during a particularly hot passage in the fighting.

After one of the volleys Colonel Udom and his Litovsk Lifeguards actually charged the cavalry with their bayonets. The guardsmen were 'in no mood to give quarter'.[5] In fact the Lifeguards lost fewer men to the enemy cuirassiers than to the horse artillery, which fired gales of grape shot through the massed ranks in the intervals between the cavalry charges. The colonel of the Izmail Regiment records that 'the enemy fire destroyed our ranks, but failed to produce any disorder among the men. The lines simply closed up again and maintained their discipline as coolly as if they had been on a musketry exercise.'[6]

The ordeal was ended by General Kretov, who galloped up with a scratch force of half-a-dozen cavalry regiments and chased Nansouty's men back over the Semenovka.

While the cavalry were battling on either flank of Semenovskaya the 2nd Combined Grenadier managed to form a ragged line just in front of the village. General Dokhturov stood beside a drum a little to the rear, calmly supervising the defence, and he fed the Moscow and Astrakhan Regiments through the ruins to the support of the grenadiers.

It says a lot for the morale of the grenadiers that they were able to 'come to life' again after being ridden over by a corps of Napoleonic cavalry. Friant's infantrymen were certainly impressed. One of the French colonels ordered his regiment to fall back, but 'at this critical moment Murat ran up to him, seized him by the collar and yelled: "What are you doing?" The colonel gestured towards the ground nearby, which was covered with the bodies of half his men, and replied: "You see we cannot possibly hang on here." "Well," cried Murat, "I'm hanging on for one!" These words stopped the colonel in his tracks. He looked Murat in the eye and spoke calmly: "You are quite right. Soldiers, face front! Let's go and get killed!" '7

In the face of Friant's new attack the gallant Russian defence at last caved in. Dufour and his 15th Regiment of Light Infantry swept over the ruins of the village, and a sizeable breach was finally effected in perhaps the most vital sector of the Russian line – the one that lay directly in line with the intact French reserve.

Meanwhile a strange silence reigned at Shevardino, where Napoleon sat amid the columns of the Old Guard. His household officers stood a little distance away ready to mount horse at his command. Sometimes he summoned Berthier for a consultation, or walked slowly up and down with his hands behind his back, but for most of the time he was rooted to his chair, peering through his pocket telescope at the smoke and dust in front, and listening impassively to the stream of adjutants, staff officers and generals who galloped from the fighting, doffed their hats and made their reports from the saddle. A brief reply and they were sent on their way with a dismissive gesture. Major Boulart of the Guard Artillery testifies that in past battles the officers were in the habit of looking on with admiration 'while the Emperor produced spectacular effects by one of his characteristic military masterstrokes. Now we lived in hope of seeing his face light up with exultation, as it did in his heyday when he announced some new miracle. But on this occasion we waited in vain!'8

Murat and Ney were left to their own devices to conduct the battle on the right, and on at least two occasions the progressive disintegration of the Russian Second West Army inspired them to send officers to the Emperor to ask him to commit the Young Guard to the battle. After the first call Napoleon debated within himself for a time, and finally gave the command for the Young Guard to set off. It had hardly marched a few yards when he ordered a halt. General Lobau contrived to shuffle the guardsmen a little way towards the fighting, on the pretext of rectifying their alignment, but Napoleon noticed the movement and ordered Lobau to stop.

General Belliard brought the second appeal at about noon. Napoleon was still cogitating whether to take the plunge when news came that the Russians were consolidating the wreckage of their regiments behind the Semenovka. Almost eagerly the Emperor told Belliard that 'before I commit my reserves I must be able to see more clearly on my chess board'. Ney was disgusted when he heard of Napoleon's caution and exclaimed that he ought to retire to the Tuileries and leave the fighting to the real generals. Murat received the news in a more charitable frame of mind, for he was aware of Napoleon's state of mental and physical exhaustion.

Thus Dokhturov and Konovnitsyn were granted a precious respite, which they used to draw up what was left of the Second West Army on the plateau behind Semenovskaya. More important still, Barclay was able to seal off the southern flank of the First West Army by moving Ostermann-Tolstoy's IV Corps down from the right to a position north-east of Semenovskaya. This movement, a purely defensive one, was elevated by the French marshals (and French historians) to the status of a full 'counter-attack'. Napoleon himself was sufficiently impressed to release some of his precious reserve, and the order went to General Sorbier to take all sixty pieces of the Guard Reserve Artillery and deploy them in support of Friant.

Sorbier rode ahead and ordered the artillery to follow him at the trot, and 'immediately the two thousand horses got this imposing mass of ordnance under way with a clanking of chains and ironwork, and dragged the guns down the side of the valley, across the floor and up the gentle further slope, which was covered with captured enemy entrenchments. At the top the team broke into a gallop so as to win the space needed for the deployment of the guns.'[10]

After his disappointment over the reinforcements, Murat and his cavalry skirmishers had been surrounded by a crowd of delighted cossacks who cried out: *'Hurrah! Hurrah! Murat!''* Murat held his admirers at a distance by slashing to right and left with his sabre, then broke through to the main body of his cavalry to give the orders for the support of the Guard artillery.

While Murat's cavalry held off the Russian horse by a series of brilliant charges, Sorbier's gunners unlimbered and opened a devastating enfilade fire against Tolstoy's infantry which was still moving to its assigned position. 'The troops advanced by thick masses, in which our roundshot ploughed wide and deep holes; they kept on coming until the French batteries redoubled their fire and crushed them by canister. Entire platoons fell simultaneously, and we could see the soldiers trying to restore their ranks under this dreadful fire,[11]. The Russians remained immobile in this position for two hours, during which time the only movement was the stirring in the lines caused by falling bodies.

Thus the combat around the Bagration Flèches and Semenovskaya ended in a bloody and spectacular manner, entirely in keeping with the scale of the battle as a whole. The *Grande Armée* had undoubtedly won the advantage on this part of the field, but by deciding to withhold the Guard, Napoleon had missed his chance of finishing off the Russian army and the war there and then.

What were the reasons for this uncharacteristic lack of decision? The Emperor was certainly functioning well below his best that day, but he himself drew attention to other considerations which would have justified caution and immobility in any ordinary general – if not in somebody of the calibre of Napoleon himself. He had to bear in mind that he was a parvenu sovereign, stranded deep in a hostile land, and that his authority rested ultimately on the preservation of a *corps d'élite*, the Imperial Guard, which was utterly devoted to his person. More immediately he appreciated that there were problems on the field of battle, his 'chessboard', which re-

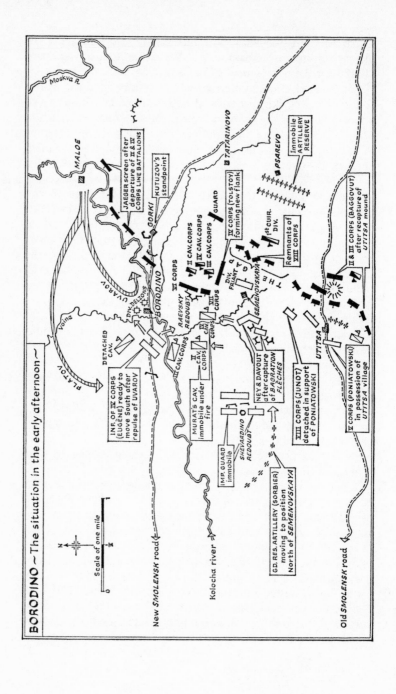

BORODINO ~ The situation in the early afternoon ~

Moskva R.

MALOE

Scale of one mile

New *SMOLENSK* road

Kolocha river

Old *SMOLENSK* road

JAEGER screen after departure of II & IV CORPS LINE BATTALIONS

KUTUZOV'S standpoint

GORKI

TATARINOVO

PSAREVO

Immobile ARTILLERY RESERVE

IV CORPS (TOLSTOY) forming new flank

1st CUIR. DIV.

II CAV.CORPS

IV CAV.CORPS

III CAV.CORPS GUARD

Remnants of VIII CORPS

II & III CORPS (BAGGOVUT) after recapture of UTITSA mound

VI CORPS

DIV. FRIANT

SEMENOVSKAYA

VII CORPS

INF. OF IV CORPS (EUGÈNE) ready to move South after repulse of UVAROV

UVAROV

DIV. DELZONS

BORODINO

RAEVSKY REDOUBT

IV CAV. CORPS

III CAV. CORPS

I CAV.CORPS

DETACHED CAV.

Voina

PLATOV

NEY & DAVOUT after capture of BAGRATION FLÈCHES

UTITSA

MURAT'S CAV. immobile under fire

VIII CORPS (JUNOT) detached in support of PONIATOWSKI

V CORPS (PONIATOWSKI) in possession of UTITSA village

IMP. GUARD immobile

SHEVARDINO REDOUBT

GD. RES. ARTILLERY (SORBIER) moving to position North of *SEMENOVSKAYA* mained unresolved: there was the uncertainty regarding the fate of Poniatowski's outflanking movement, which had presumably become bogged down at Utitsa; more important still, the cavalry on the Russian far right had embarked on an unexpected and wide-ranging expedition which seemed to threaten the security of the whole *Grande Armée*[12].

V

Uvarov's diversion.

At daybreak on 7 September the lower reaches of the Kolocha river were honoured by the attention of Matvei Ivanovich Platov, General of Cavalry and Ataman of the Don Cossacks, who was prospecting for fords. Not only did Platov discover what he was looking for, but he perceived that the French had left the far bank totally unguarded.

Immediately he sent off a young volunteer, the Prince of Hessen-Philippsthal, to tell Kutuzov of the discovery and suggest that the powerful cavalry of the Russian right should cross by the ford and fall on the enemy flank. On his way to Gorki the Prince met the clever Colonel Toll, who was very taken with the scheme and promised to put it to the generalissimo. He came at the right moment, for headquarters had just received news of the recapture of the Raevsky Redoubt from Morand's division. Toll suggested that the whole of the cavalry of the Russian right should be committed to the attack, to which Kutuzov simply replied '*Eh bien! Prenez-le!*'

So far the whole weight of the French attack had fallen on the centre and left of the Russian line, and until the late morning no part of the Russian armies had spent its time less usefully than the eight thousand cavalrymen who were marooned on the far right. These consisted of the 2,500 regular cavalry of Lieutenant-General F. P. Uvarov's I Cavalry Corps, thirty-six pieces of horse artillery and Platov's 5,500 cossacks. The Russian high command was delighted at the prospect of putting them to good use, and Barclay began to talk of dealing the enemy 'a decisive blow'.[1]

Uvarov and Platov moved forward at about eleven o'clock and forded the Kolocha near Maloe. They cautiously negotiated the potentially dangerous gap between Borodino and the woods to the north, and bore slowly down on the Italian and Bavarian cavalry of Count Ornano, which extended in a thin screen on the far left of the *Grande Armée*. The mass of yellow-clad hussars, dark green dragoons and blue and red cossacks flooded over Ornano's command and the Bavarian horse artillery had to make off in some haste, losing two guns to the Elisabetgrad Hussars.

Platov's cossacks went on to cross the Voina stream on a wide frontage and roam about in the French rear, but the impetus of Uvarov's regular cavalry was checked by the infantry division of General Delzons, which formed up in squares to the north of Borodino and incorporated the remnants of Ornano's cavalry. The Elisabetgrad Hussars charged three times but failed to produce any wavering in the ranks. Powerful bodies of French cavalry now began to arrive on the scene from the south, and the regimental columns of the 6th Hussars and 8th *Chasseurs-à-Cheval* played havoc with the Russian cuirassiers 'for they were armoured only on their chests, and so we could do great execution by thrusting at them as they fled'.[2]

The Russian cavalry fell back to the Kolocha (losing its two captured cannon in the process), and, after standing its ground for a time, withdrew to the east bank in the afternoon.

As seen from the main Russian positions the whole performance was deeply disappointing. It appeared to Barclay and General Löwenstern that Uvarov and Platov had advanced with disgraceful slowness, and that the whole course of the subsequent fighting had gone plainly against the Russian horse. The artillery officer Rodozhitsky records that while his battery was moving along the east side of the Kolocha 'we heard a loud noise of musketry to our right, which came from the French infantry which was firing at our cavalry, and then suddenly a number of scattered hussars galloped past us. Several of them had been shot through, and fell from their horses on the way; among them was a splendid officer, who had been hit in the chest and toppled from the saddle two yards to our front.'[3]

Uvarov returned to a chilly reception. Kutuzov heard him out then simply remarked: 'I know. May God forgive you!'[4] As for the feeble performance of Platov, Ermolov remarked that 'it is a general rule that cossacks are of little use in an open battle, and the same held true here, when they came back after encountering a few obstructions'.[5] Captain Murav'ev suggests that the cossacks deliberately hung back because they disliked being attached to the army of the 'German' Barclay, whom they hated 'even more than we did'.[6]

It was only after the war, when the historian D. N. Bolgovsky questioned the French commanders, that the Russians began to appreciate just how much they owed to Platov and Uvarov. For more than two hours, from mid-day until after two in the afternoon, the diversion had effectively paralysed the French left and centre. The wounded in the dressing station at the Kolotskoi Monastery were thrown into an understandable panic at the report that the cossacks were on the loose, and as far south as Shevardino the Imperial Guard made ready to receive any cavalry which might attack from the rear. Napoleon was confirmed in his reluctance to commit his reserve to exploiting the break-through at Semenovskaya, while Eugène had to postpone a new attack which he had in store for the Raevsky Redoubt. Altogether seventeen cavalry regiments were committed to the left bank of the Kolocha in order to shore up the left flank of the *Grande Armée*,[7] which left Grouchy with only four cavalry regiments on the south bank. Eugène crossed the stream to supervise affairs in person, and Napoleon himself rode some way to the left and did not return to his Shevardino vantage point until three in the afternoon. For much of this time Latour-Maubourg's cavalrymen stood immobile under the guns of the Raevsky Redoubt, and they suffered hideously in the process.

If Kutuzov had done nothing else at Borodino, he would have justified his presence by unleashing the diversion against the French left. Having said that, we have to face the uncomfortable truth that there *was* very little else that Kutuzov did in the course of the battle. He cut a strangely unimpressive figure in his round white forage cap and his dark green overcoat without epaulettes. He spent most of the time seated amid a litter of bottles and food, and occasionally went for short excursions on his distinctive white horse, a powerful beast with a long tail. Ermolov comments bitterly that when Morand's division began to move against the Raevsky Redoubt 'I was with Kutuzov on a battery on the right flank, so far removed from danger that the enemy did not honour it with a single shot until it was almost evening'.[8]

Thus Barclay and Bagration were left to manage affairs largely by themselves, and Kutuzov's interventions, such as they were, proved to be well-intentioned but arbitrary. Barclay had religiously abided by the prohibition against any premature laying of hands upon the reserves, and he was astonished when General Löwenstern told him early in the battle that Kutuzov had sent away the Izmail and Litovsk Lifeguards to support the Second West Army. 'Barclay was aroused from his ordinary equanimity, his eyes blazed with anger and he exclaimed: "It seems that Kutuzov and General Bennigsen think that the battle is played out, when it is really scarce begun. I did not count on putting in my reserve before five or six in the evening, but they have used it up by ten in the morning." '[9]

At times it appears that the only reasonably well-informed person on the battlefield was that congenital busybody, Colonel Toll.

In fairness we should quote the opinion of Friedrich von Schubert, an officer on Barclay's staff, who took it on himself to defend Kutuzov against the denigrators 'who laughed at the convenient and safe place he had chosen for himself'.[10] Schubert argued that Kutuzov could have done no real good in the thick of the fighting, and that his death would have deprived the Russians of the one man who could and would take the vast responsibility of the battle upon himself; as for the management of the combat Kutuzov knew that he could leave affairs in the hands of Barclay and the 'reliable' Chief-of-Staff, Bennigsen.

VI

The Fall of the Raevsky Redoubt

The enforced suspension of the *Grande Armée*'s attacks proved particularly disagreeable to Murat's cavalrymen, who were moved north at about noon to plug the gap between the infantry around Semenovskaya and Eugène's IV Corps, which was now fully committed to warding off Uvarov's diversion. The result was that for the best part of three hours these expensive and glittering horsemen sat almost immobile within range of the guns of the Raevsky Redoubt.

The Saxon cavalry brigade lost about half its men in the battle, and most of them fell during these few hours. Roth von Schreckenstein comments that 'for healthy, strong men who are mounted on good horses a cavalry battle is nothing compared with what Napoleon made his cavalry put up with at Borodino . . . to hold out inactively under fire . . . must be one of the most unpleasant things cavalry can be called on to do . . . there can have been scarcely a man in those ranks and files whose neighbour did not crash to earth with his horse, or die from terrible wounds while screaming for help'.[1] General Griois noticed that there was 'a regiment of Württemberg cuirassiers near me which seemed to have been singled out as a special target, and their shattered helmets and cuirasses flew in splinters through the whole formation. Some French carabiniers had been posted further ahead, and they too suffered heavily, especially from musketry, the balls ringing out when they struck their armour.'[2]

Among the Germans the brigade commander, Lieutenant-General Thielemann, barely escaped a roundshot which killed his adjutant and a trumpeter and beheaded the horse of a nearby officer. The general's own horse was wounded by a splinter, and his nerves were so ragged that when a Polish officer annoyed him he chased the wretched man some distance with his drawn sword.

No. II Reserve Cavalry Corps suffered the loss of its popular commander, General Louis-Pierre Montbrun, who was trying to move Pajol's division under some kind of cover when a shell splinter hit him in the stomach. 'A good shot!' he exclaimed, then, turning pale, sank from the saddle in front of his horrified cavalrymen. He was carried from the field and died at five o'clock. Napoleon chose one of his own aides-de-camp, General Auguste de Caulaincourt, to help direct the battered cavalry and sent him on the way with the injunction: 'Do as you did as Arzobispo!' – a reference to an episode of 8 August, 1809, when Caulaincourt had forced the passage of the Tagus with a detachment of dragoons.

It was some consolation that the French gunners were bringing the Raevsky Redoubt under a cross-fire from 170 pieces at Borodino and Semenovskaya. The air above the battery was crackling with premature shell-bursts, but enough shot and shell struck the fortification to pound the breastwork

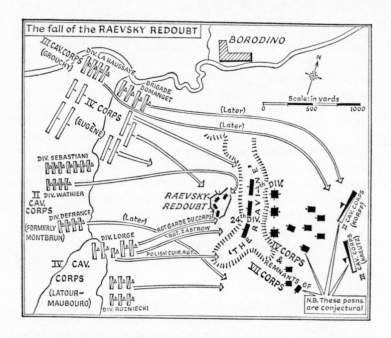

The fall of the RAEVSKY REDOUBT

BORODINO

III CAV. CORPS (GROUCHY)

DIV. LA HAUSSAYE

BRIGADE DOMANGET

IV CORPS (EUGÈNE)

(Later)

(Later)

N

Scale: in yards
0   500   1000

DIV. SEBASTIANI

II CAV. CORPS

DIV. WATHIER

RAEVSKY REDOUBT

7th DIV.

II CAV. CORPS (KORFF)

DIV. DEFRANCE

(FORMERLY MONTBRUN)

DIV. LORGE

(Later)

RGT. GARDE DU CORPS

RGT. ZASTROW

24th DIV.

THE RAVINE

I CAV. CORPS (KREUTZ)

IV CAV. CORPS (LATOUR-MAUBOURG)

POLISH CUIR. RGT.

DIV. ROZNIECKI

IV CORPS & REMNANTS OF VII CORPS

N.B. These posns. are conjectural.

---

into a shapeless mass and practically fill the ditch with sand.
In the rear of the battery a shell ignited a barrel filled with
resin, which the Russians employed to lubricate the axles of
their guns, and 'the purple flames rolled along the ground like
an infuriated snake, then climbed upwards in columns of
smoke, throwing broad shadows on the ground'.[3] A nearby
battery of horse artillery lost 93 of its men and 113 horses in
less than an hour.

As always the immediate defence of the redoubt was left
to the gunners, and the infantry were standing to the rear in
battalion columns: old Major-General Likhachev's 24th
Division of VI Corps was positioned closest to the redoubt,
with Kaptsevich's 7th Division (also of VI Corps) a little to
the right. Tolstoy's IV Corps formed the left flank of the positions around the Raevsky Redoubt, and indeed of the Russian
army as a whole, now that Bagration's old command had
virtually disappeared.

Some time after three in the afternoon the French began
to prepare for the long-postponed attack on the Raevsky

Redoubt. Three of Eugène's infantry divisions, those of Broussier, Morand and Gérard, were drawn up south of the Kolocha, though it was a moot point whether they would be able to reach the target before the powerful force of cavalry that was massing on their right. This consisted of II Reserve Cavalry Corps, immediately opposite the redoubt, and Latour-Maubourg's IV Reserve Cavalry Corps, a short distance to the south.

Barclay noticed that the *Grande Armée* was coalescing in columns in front of the Redoubt, and he foresaw 'that they were going to launch a ferocious attack. I immediately sent for the 1st Cuirassier Division, supposing it was still in the place I had assigned for it [i.e. in the reserve behind the Lifeguard Division], for I had intended to hoard it for a decisive blow. Unfortunately someone, I don't know who, had moved it to the extreme left flank. All my adjutant could do was to collect just two regiments of Lifeguard Cuirassiers and bring them to me by companies as fast as he was able.'[4] By then the enemy was already on the move, and Barclay refused to let his cuirassiers go in against such odds. For some time, therefore, the gunners and the supporting infantry would have to defend the redoubt by themselves.

The French infantry moved off just before three in the afternoon. On the right flank the cuirassiers of IV Corps were fuming with impatience, but at last a staff officer galloped up to Thielemann and announced: 'On behalf of the Emperor I bring you the order to attack!'[5]

The cavalry of both corps rapidly overhauled the dark-blue columns of French infantry to the left, and 'the whole eminence which overhung us appeared in an instant a mass of moving iron: the glitter of arms, and the rays of the sun, reflected from the helmets and cuirasses of the dragoons, mingled with the flames of the cannon that on every side vomited forth death, to give the appearance of a volcano in the midst of the army.'[6] An enormous plume of smoke and dust arose from the redoubt, and drew the attention of the whole Russian army to the struggle that was going on there. An officer who was standing near Gorki reports that 'the brilliant rays of the half-hidden sun were reflected from the sabres, swords, bayonets, helmets and cuirasses, making a dreadful yet sublime picture . . . . Already the French were under the redoubt itself, and our cannon gave a final salvo—then fell silent. A dull cheering told us that the enemy had burst over the rampart and were going to work with the bayonet'.[7]

The race to the Redoubt was probably won by Wathier's division of cuirassiers, who were about to burst in from the rear when they were driven off by a devastating volley delivered by the supporting infantry at a range of sixty yards. General Caulaincourt was at the head of the 5th Cuirassiers and he had almost reached the northern gap in the palisade when he was killed by a musket bullet under the heart.

The repulse of Wathier's division left the field clear for IV Reserve Cavalry Corps, which was advancing against the southern flank of the redoubt. Thielemann had formed Lorge's cuirassier division in a neat column for the attack, but while the cavalry pounded up the gentle slope the Garde du Corps drew out to the left and made directly for the breastwork of the battery, which gradually unmasked the Zastrow Cuirassiers.

The Garde du Corps and the nearest squadrons of the Zastrows poured into the sand- and corpse-filled ditch, and the best riders scrambled over the breastwork, while the others forced their way through the embrasures or tried to work their way around to the rear. Soon 'the cramped interior space of the redoubt was filled with a frightful press of murderously-intentioned cavalry and Russian infantry [sic], thrown pell-mell together and doing their best to throttle and mangle one another.'[8] The rearward regiments and the rest of the Zastrow squadrons poured into the redoubt by the southern entrance or rode directly against the infantry lurking in the ravine behind.

The very first stride over the lip of the ravine carried the Saxon cavalrymen into a compact mass of uplifted bayonets, while they were greeted from the far side by a volley of whistling bullets. Many of the riders were shot from the saddle and rolled to the bottom of the ravine and on top of the Russian wounded, which gave rise to a macabre struggle on the ground among the men who could still move. They did what damage they could to one another with swords, fists and teeth until the

126

rearward ranks of cavalry charged down with wild cries, 'trampling everything under the hooves of their horses and throwing themselves infuriatedly on the Russian masses behind. Wherever the cavalrymen burst through they did not bother whether anyone was able to follow them, but stormed up the steep further slope to the far edge, where the rest of the infantry calmly awaited them with levelled bayonets.'[9]

While the cavalry rampaged inside the Redoubt and swirled around outside, the French infantrymen made their way uphill to consolidate the conquest. As they broke into the Redoubt they found that the parapets were half battered down and the embrasures completely destroyed. The inside was a mass of broken gun carriages and other débris. Labaume writes that 'in the midst of this scene of carnage I discovered the body of a Russian cannoneer decorated with three crosses. In one hand he held a broken sword, and with the other he firmly grasped the carriage of the gun at which he had so valiantly fought.'[10] According to a Polish officer it was 'quite impossible to describe the impression made by the sight of the Raevsky Redoubt . . . there were dead and mutilated men and horses lying six or eight deep. Their bodies covered the whole area of the entrances. They filled the ditch and were heaped up inside the fortification. While we were still advancing towards the redoubt . . . several cuirassiers came by, carrying General Caulaincourt on a white cuirassier cloak which was stained with great blotches of blood.

'By the breastwork there was an elderly staff officer, leaning against one of the guns with a gaping wound in the head [possibly the same hero mentioned by Labaume]. Most of the dead along the front of the Redoubt were infantrymen. On the right-hand-side of the Redoubt and in the work itself there were the bodies of cuirassiers in white and blue uniforms— Saxon Gardes du Corps, Zastrow Cuirassiers, and men from the 5th and, if I am not mistaken, also the 8th Cuirassier Regiments.'[11]

The sick and aged General Likhachev was among the few prisoners. He had thrown himself despairingly against the French, who rescued the brave old man from their own bayonets and carried him to the rear. Surprisingly enough in all this turmoil the Russians managed to extricate six guns from the Redoubt. They had to abandon two more at the northern entrance, and they heaved a third into the ditch.

The capture of a large battery by virtually unsupported cavalry was a brilliant feat of arms, and we now know that the credit almost certainly belongs to Lorge's cuirassiers. These well-deserving Saxons and Poles were bitterly disappointed to learn from an eyewitness that Napoleon attributed the victory to Wathier's French cuirassiers. 'Napoleon was standing beside Berthier,' so the account ran, 'when the latter looked through his telescope and exclaimed: "The Redoubt has been taken! The Saxon cuirassiers are inside!" Napoleon had evidently picked up the same telescope and he replied: "You are mistaken, They are dressed in blue and they must be *my* cuirassiers." '[12] The Emperor had forgotten that the Polish cuirassiers were uniformed very much like the French, and that one of the Westphalian regiments also sported blue jackets. Posterity is still wider of the mark when it attributes the whole of the charge to Caulaincourt, who at the most functioned as a brigade commander in Wathier's division.

After the reduction of the Raevsky Redoubt Prince Eugène gathered all the available cavalry of the *Grande Armée*, including Grouchy's corps, and threw them at the already badly-battered Russian infantry standing behind the fortification, namely the 7th Division and Tolstoy's IV Corps.

The Russians were drawn up on the plateau in a first line of three squadrons and a reserve of several battalion columns. The Napoleonic cavalry penetrated the gaps of this deceptively open formation and surged around the blocks of Russian infantry. At some points the officers managed to push their horses through the compact ranks and open the way for a few men to follow, but the rest of the cavalry simply raged up and down the hedge of bayonets, futilely slashing with their swords. The *Grande Armée* had learnt the uselessness of such tactics in the campaign of 1809, but in the heat of the battle the German cavalry now forgot everything they had been taught about lunging downwards against infantry with the point of the sword. Every now and again they saw the horrid picture of the Russians raising their muskets to their shoulders, and then the bullets would 'screech like rockets around our ears'.[13]

22 A Russian 10-pounder (system of 1805) outside the Borodino museum.
(Novosti Press Agency)

23 The Museum of Military History at Borodino. *(Novosti Press Agency)*

24 The Battle of Borodino Panorama Building in Moscow. *(Novosti Press Agency)*

25 Part of the Borodino Panorama painted by F. Rubo. *(Novosti Press Agency)*

Barclay was in the process of feeding his own cavalry into the fighting, and 'now began one of the most stubborn cavalry battles of history'.[14] The Russian Lifeguard Cavalry was first on the scene, and threw itself without more ado on Defrance's division of cuirassiers. Major-General Korff brought the II Cavalry Corps up in support, and soon his Iziumsk Hussars and Polish Lancers were pitted in an unequal struggle against no less than eight regiments of cuirassiers and carabiniers. The Courlanders of the splendid Pskov Dragoons hewed their way through to the assistance of their comrades, and helped to prolong the struggle until the Russian III Cavalry Corps intervened.

During this two-hour battle on the plateau the Russian and French cavalry regiments became almost inextricably mixed up with each other and with the remnants of the Russian infantry, and in some places the dust was kicked up in such dense clouds that no one could see more than ten yards. To add to the horror of the scene 'hordes of riderless horses were neighing with terror and ran with streaming manes among the dead and wounded.'[15] The Russian infantry commanders did what they could to rally their men amid the confusion. General Paskevich charged up and down, tearing out his hair and swearing. Just as characteristically Barclay retained his composure through the whole chapter of alarming episodes: at one time his horse was shot beneath him and he had to seek refuge in a square of infantry; at another his loyal groom raised a pistol and shot a French cuirassier from the saddle just as the man was about to split his master's head in two.

During the great cavalry battle the rival batteries kept up a heavy fire against whatever targets happened to present themselves. Coloned Prince Kudashev raked the last of Grouchy's reserves to enter the fight with his four pieces of Lifeguard Horse Artillery, while further Russian batteries concentrated their fire against the rear of the Raevsky Redoubt, virtually levelling it to the ground.

Even so there were many Russian guns which never saw action, such was the disruption caused by Kutaisov's death in the chain of artillery command. Captain Figner's company of light artillery was stationed uselessly behind a regiment of dragoons somewhere to the rear of the Raevsky Redoubt, and

Rodozhitsky, one of the officers, had ample time to take in the scene: 'we could see several dead Russian soldiers and one blown-up ammunition cart, which was surrounded by a patch of burnt grass and the charred remains of the horses and drivers.' To his right there were a few survivors of the crews of four pieces of horse artillery, and immediately to his front the dragoons came under heavy fire. 'Shot, shell, canister and even musket balls flew through the files of the dragoons and among our gunners, striking down several men and horses. Here I appreciated the truth that nothing is less pleasant on a battlefield than to stand inactive under enemy fire: almost every solder followed the flight of the cannon shot with his eyes and paid them a degree of involuntary respect.' Rodozhitsky turned to Figner and begged him to get the guns into action, but 'I had not finished what I wanted to say when something flew by my left temple and knocked me from my horse.'

Rodozhitsky had been concussed by a shell splinter, and he joined the stream of wounded who were being assisted to the rear by peasants and the Moscow *opolchenie*. At the dressing station he encountered 'a great number of other unfortunates, with various wounds, who were emitting groans and yells. There was a Tartar who was a particularly horrifying and pitiable case . . . as I came in the surgeons were extracting a bullet from his back, causing him to writhe and scream in a frightful manner.'[16]

On the other side of the field the surgeons of the *Grande Armée* were also hard at work. No one had told them in advance where to collect the wounded, contrary to the practice in most of Napoleon's battles, and after patching up the men as best they could they sent them to the regimental camps, the neighbouring villages or to the already overcrowded main dressing station at the Kolotskoi Monastery.

VII

The final stages of the battle

By five in the afternoon the fury of the great cavalry battle on the plateau behind the Redoubt had largely abated. To the Russian staff officer, Carl von Clausewitz, it seemed 'most striking how the action gradually reflected the weariness and exhaustion of the armies. The masses of infantry had melted away so drastically that perhaps less than one-third of the original number was still in action: the rest of the troops were dead, wounded, engaged in carrying away the casualties or rallying in the rear. Everywhere there were wide gaps. The mighty artillery . . . now spoke only by sporadic shots, and even these did not seem to ring out in the old strong and thunderous style, but sounded languid and muffled. The cavalry had almost everywhere taken the place of the infantry, and it moved up and down in a tired trot.'[1]

Barclay had lost all but three of his adjutants, and he saved himself from physical collapse only by drinking a glass of rum and bolting a scrap of bread. He never took his eye off the enemy movements and waited for the moment when Napoleon would throw in his reserve and decide the battle.

Napoleon had no such intention. 'I will not have my Guard destroyed,' he exclaimed. 'When you are eight hundred leagues from France you do not wreck your last reserve.' Berthier and Bessières were in full agreement, and this time even Murat supported Napoleon's reasoning.

At this juncture the captured General Likhachev was brought before the Emperor, which presented him with a magnificent opportunity to finish off the day with a theatrically generous gesture. Napoleon took up what he supposed to be the Russian's weapon and proffered it with the words 'I return you your sword'. Likhachev stood dumb and motionless, for he had never seen the sword before. For a moment Napoleon was thunderstruck, then he shrugged his shoulders and turned to his entourage with the remark: 'Take this idiot away!'[2]

Now that the Imperial Guard had been finally withheld from the battle, the only troops with any fight left in them were on the extreme southern flank of the field, around Utitsa, where Poniatowski's Poles and Baggovut's Russians were still waging their private war.

After three hours of artillery duelling Poniatowski heard of the capture of the Raevsky Redoubt, and decided to launch a two-pronged attack on the Russian positions around the Utitsa mound. Two columns of infantry advanced around the northern flank of the hill until they were stopped short by the bayonets of the Brest, Ryazan, Willmanstrand and Minsk infantry regiments and the pikes of five hundred of the Moscow *opolchenie*. As a diversion, however, the left-hand attack proved outstandingly successful, and Poniatowski's main force of infantry and cavalry made good progress to the south of the hill. Baggovut staved off collapse only by throwing Karpov's cossacks, the 1st Grenadier Division and the 17th Infantry Division into a counter-attack.

By the late afternoon the main Russian army had ceded so much ground that Baggovut was left holding a dangerously exposed salient. He therefore fell back some distance along the Old Smolensk Road and abandoned the Utitsa mound to the Poles. The retreat was taken amiss by some of the generals, and Baggovut reluctantly gave Prince Eugene permission to make a suicidal attempt to recover the height with the survivors of the Kremenchug and Minsk regiments. These 650 men were almost immediately engulfed by the enemy, and he fought his way back to the main Russian position with a depleted force of scarcely 350.

By now the Russians had been driven from almost the entire length of their original line of battle, and as the evening mist rose Barclay sent Wolzogen to Kutuzov to tell him of the desperate situation and ask for reinforcements. Knowing the generalissimo's sly habits as he did, Barclay was careful to stipulate that any instructions should be given in writing: 'You cannot be too careful when you are dealing with Kutuzov.' Wolzogen rode some distance without being able to find Kutuzov, but 'at last I discovered him half an hour's journey behind the army on the New Smolensk Road, surrounded by a suite so numerous that it looked to me like an entire corps of reinforcements. This entourage consisted almost entirely of young, rich Russian officers of the most prominent families, who had been enjoying every kind of pleasure and had taken no part whatsoever in the dreadfully serious events of that day. Colonel Toll was there as well, tucking into a capon.

'I duly embarked on my report concerning the position and state of the Russian Army, and I explained that apart from the right wing, which was on and to the left of the Smolensk Road, we had lost all our important positions and that every regiment was in a state of extreme exhaustion and disarray. I was

132

still speaking when Kutuzov cut me short with the cry: "You must have been getting drunk with some flea-bitten sutler woman to give me a report like that! We have victoriously repulsed the French attacks along the whole length of our front, and to-morrow I shall place myself at the head of the army and drive the enemy without more ado from the holy soil of Russia!" With that he looked around challengingly at the members of his suite, who nodded in enthusiastic approval.'[3]

Wolzogen was all the angrier at his reception because he knew that Kutuzov had spent the battle 'in the rear of the army surrounded by champagne bottles and eating delicacies.' Choking down his indignation, he replied that Kutuzov could take his report any way he wished, but that he must have written orders to carry to Barclay. The generalissimo conferred a few minutes with Toll, then dictated an order which told Barclay to withdraw the army about one thousand yards to a rearward position which was to be aligned with the hill of Gorki on the right and the Utitsa woods on the left. 'From all the enemy movements,' continued Kutuzov, 'I see that they have suffered just as much in the battle as we have. I therefore intend to continue the action. I shall restore the army to order during the night and replenish the artillery with ammunition, so that we may renew the battle to-morrow. If we withdrew in our present disorderly state we would lose all our artillery.'[4] The same orders were sent to Dokhturov, as acting commander of what was left of the Second West Army.

Wolzogen carried the instructions back to Barclay, who 'shook his head and told me: "I don't know whether we could ever summon up the strength. It might even be easier to go out straightaway and attack the French where they are. By to-morrow morning a new attack will be almost out of the question, because the soldiers will be so exhausted. They have already gone without food for twelve hours of great exertion, and there is no hope of any more food reaching them during the night." '[5]

The Russians fell back at about six in the evening. The retreat brought the army to the position of the reserve artillery, which was still largely intact, and according to Kutuzov 'a ferocious artillery duel lasted until it was completely dark. Our artillery caused immense damage with its roundshot and compelled the enemy batteries to fall silent, after which all the French infantry and cavalry withdrew.'[6] Kutuzov still believed that he had won a resounding defensive victory, and he sent a report to this effect to the Tsar by the hand of a jaeger who had been in Mozhaisk throughout the battle and consequently had no idea of what had really happened. The despatch caused much rejoicing in St Petersburg, and Alexander sent Kutuzov a gift of 100,000 roubles and announced his promotion to field-marshal.

After the troops had taken up the new line Kutuzov sent Colonel Toll and another of his adjutants, A. B. Golitsyn, to investigate the condition of the army. They found that the artillery had shot away most of its ammunition, and that many of the gun carriages were so damaged that they had to be bound together with rope. It soon transpired that the infantry was in an even worse state. At one point Toll encountered Colonel Khomentovsky at the head of a small band of men and asked: 'What regiment is that?' the colonel simply replied: 'They are the 2nd Division.'[7] Raevsky could muster only seven hundred men of his VII Corps under arms, and it was evident that the First and Second West Armies together would be able to put no more than 45,000 troops into the field next day.

At about half-past-ten Toll returned to the headquarters at Tatarino and reported to Kutuzov. The generalissimo thereupon turned to his commanders and announced that he had decided to retreat the following morning. As he reported later to the Tsar, taking into consideration 'the losses and disorder in our battalions after this bloody battle, as well as the superior force of the enemy, I resolved to retreat on the height near Mozhaisk so as to consolidate the army.'[8] He designated Major-General Korff as commander of the cavalry rearguard, and sent one of his many adjutants to rouse Barclay from his exhausted sleep at Gorki.

Golitsyn claims that Kutuzov never had any intention of giving battle the next day, but merely kept up a bellicose front until Toll's report gave him a convenient excuse to 'change his mind'.[9] This supposition certainly fits in with what we know of Kutuzov's character, though his first report to the Tsar was couched in such optimistic terms that we cannot accept Golitsyn's story without reservation.

Compared with the immense physical damage suffered by the Russian army, the loss or gain of the field of battle itself was of no importance. Indeed the French too fell back some distance under cover of night, and on the southern flank Baggovut 'sent out a party of cossacks to observe the enemy withdrawal. They returned with the report that the French had retreated beyond the Kolocha.'[10] Before long the whole field was swarming with cossacks, and in the darkness a party of them speared two Russian officers who were unwise enough to be talking French. On the right Captain Murav'ev, searching for a missing brother, discovered that the Raevsky Redoubt was 'piled high with dreadful heaps of dead and wounded'[11] but had been abandoned by the French. Barclay learnt of this and sent General Miloradovich with several battalions and a battery to re-occupy the position at daybreak.

Barclay himself rode towards the redoubt at first light and Wolzogen recalls that 'it was horrible to see that enormous mass of riddled soldiers, French and Russians were cast together, and there were many wounded men who were incapable of moving and lay in that wild chaos intermingled with the bodies of horses and the wreckage of shattered cannon.'[12]

By now the Russian baggage and reserve artillery was well advanced on the road to Mozhaisk. It was here that Kutuzov discovered that the local government of Moscow had ignored his repeated requests to have relays of waggons ready to convey the wounded back to Moscow, but somehow or other he managed to pile most of the men on the army's own carts and carry them off. Many of the missing troops had found their way back to their regiments, and the columns began to file off after the waggons and guns. The enemy showed no interest in the proceedings, apart from sending a few cannon shot bounding down the Mozhaisk road, and by ten in the morning of 8 September the evacuation of the field was complete.

The troops of the *Grande Armée* spent the night huddled over such fires as could be made from broken musket stocks or the splintered timbers of carts and gun carriages. A few men rummaged in the knapsacks of the fallen Russians, and discovered flasks of pepper-laced brandy which afforded them a little additional warmth. A sense of shock pervaded the army, and it was prolonged through the next morning when the survivors picked over the abandoned battlefield and found that 'the few places that were not encumbered with the slain, were covered with broken lances, muskets, helmets and cuirasses, or with canister and bullets, as numerous as hailstones after a violent storm.'[31]

Napoleon was overcome by a profound depression, as well being physically exhausted, and it was noon before he and his suite rode over the ground. 'Everything conspired to lend the field a dreadful aspect: a leaden sky, a cold rain driven by a violent wind, the charred ruins of the houses, and the whole ploughed-up plain which was strewn with wreckage and débris and rimmed about with the gloomy and dark trees of these northern climes. Everywhere there were soldiers wandering among the corpses and rifling for food amid the knapsacks of their dead comrades. The wounds of the fallen men were terrible, for the Russian bullets were larger than ours. Then there was the brooding silence of our camps, enlivened no longer by cheerful songs or tales.'[14] The surviving soldiers wore torn, blackened and bloody uniforms, and their officers were able to raise no more than a few thin shouts of 'victory!' for the benefit of the Emperor.

Strangest of all was the increasing sense of wonder which Napoleon's men felt for the prowess of the Russians, whose presence seemed to pervade the battlefield even though all their troops were lying dead or wounded or had already disappeared over the horizon.

Captain François was among the lucky survivors of the 30th Regiment's attack on the Raevsky Redoubt, and he admits that he 'had been in more than one campaign, but I must say that I had never yet been engaged in such a bloody mêlée or pitted against more stubborn soldiers than the Russians. I was in a dreadful state: my shako had been carried away by canister: my coat-tails had been torn off by the Russians in the hand-to-hand fighting; I had bruises everywhere, and I was suffering horribly from the wound in my left leg.'[15]

One of the Saxon cuirassiers noted that 'in our various charges we managed to capture only a few Russian cavalrymen, and I do not recall having seen a single Russian officer taken prisoner.'[16] Napoleon, too, was struck by the curious

136

lack of prisoners, and during the battle he remarked to his entourage: 'These Russians let themselves be killed like automatons; they are not taken alive. This does not help us at all. These citadels should be demolished with cannon.'[17]

These impressions were confirmed by the events of the afternoon of the 8th, when Murat launched his combined cavalry corps in tardy pursuit and was checked in a lively cavalry action outside Mozhaisk. Latour-Maubourg was full of admiration for men who could put up a stiff fight after so terrible a battle. The cavalry encountered nothing on the road which indicated the slightest haste or disorder in the retreat, and Roth von Schreckenstein testifies that 'the Russians had no alternative but to leave many dead and wounded on the battlefield, but I am of the opinion that any other army would have left behind double the number. The Russians have this peculiarity, that they do not willingly relinquish a single wounded man in battle; indeed if it is at all possible they carry the bodies of their officers away with them.'[78]

The men who were left behind showed extraordinary stoicism. The hopelessly wounded troops uttered hardly a moan, the regulars clutching for comfort at their St. Nicholas medals, while the cossacks clasped little parcels of earth from their native villages. The French officers guided their horses around these heroes only with some difficulty, and at one spot Napoleon's horse trod directly on one of the men, to the Emperor's obvious distress. If a wounded Russian could so much as crawl, he would drag himself to the nearest tree, tear off a branch, and with the help of this improvised crutch hobble off in the direction of his retreating army.

Whether the men were wounded or not, abandoned or still in the ranks, the Russian soldiers were gripped by a primitive homing instinct, an urge to draw together and consolidate which falsified all the rational calculations of Napoleon, the Westerner. On the 8th Prince Eugène and his staff were in the Raevsky Redoubt, warming themselves around a fire which they fed with the remains of a Russian gun carriage; there were bodies all around, but suddenly they saw a young Russian raise himself up among the corpses, rub his eyes, look about him in a daze, then get slowly to his feet and walk away to freedom. Nobody thought of stopping him.

137

Chapter 9

THE RECKONING

The regimental clerks in the rival armies were hard at work on the day after the battle, drawing up the lists of casualties. In one of Napoleon's German regiments they 'used a dead horse as a writing table, and the orderlies even dragged up a few Russian corpses to act as chairs for the scribes, who were re-fighting the battle with their pens.'[1]

For all the devoted scribbling twentieth-century historians still do not have enough evidence to be able to agree on the details of the butcher's bill. The Russian historian Garnich puts the losses of Kutuzov's army as low as 38,500,[2] though most other Soviet historians accept the figure of 44,000 dead and wounded as reasonable (including twenty-three generals), which amounts to about 34 per cent of the forces committed to the battle.[3]

Such casualty lists as we possess certainly bear out the impression that the fighting was heaviest along the central and southern sectors of the Russian line. The 6th Jaeger Regiment sustained the most severe losses in Bagration's Second West Army, with 910 NCOs and men reported as casualties, of whom 372 were killed. The bitterness of the struggle around Semenovskaya is attested by the fact that the units of Barclay's army which suffered most heavily were the Izmail and Litovsk Life-guards moved there from the reserve. The Litovsk Regiment lost 741 NCOs and men, compared with 777 of the Izmails, but the former suffered the greater proportion of dead – 435 to 176: probably they had come under the heavier canister fire, whereas the Izmails were cut up by the cavalry swords.

The Russians like to think that the *Grande Armée* lost 58,000 men, or about 40 per cent of the total.[4] though David Chandler in his monumental *Campaign of Napoleon* concludes that 'the *Grande Armée* certainly lost no less than 30,000 killed or wounded . . . . Marshal Davout was among the French wounded and no less than 14 lieutenant-generals and 33 major-generals were dead or wounded. The French casualty list also includes the names of 32 staff officers, 86 aides-de-camp, and 37 colonels of regiments.'[5]

One reliable set of statistics relates to the corpses of 58,521 men and 35,478 horses buried by the Russians in 1813. Many thousands more had probably been buried already, or had died from their wounds away from the battlefield. We can appreciate the feelings of the Russian officer Shcherbinin who wrote after the war that 'with the exception of the insignificant rearguard action at Vitebsk this was the first battle in which I had taken part. I supposed that every general action was fought out as bitterly as this one. Afterwards I found myself in 1812, 1813 and 1814 under the command of Toll, Konovnitsyn and Miloradovich, and I participated in a whole series of general engagements as well as a variety of other operations, and I discovered that they stood in the same relation to Borodino as peacetime manoeuvres did to the realities of war itself.'[6]

The *Grande Armée* had stood up magnificently under the severest test it had yet undergone on a battlefield. The infantry was thrown directly against prepared positions, and despite repeated repulses it returned doggedly to the attack until the Russians were finally driven from their post. However we must agree with Roth von Schreckenstein that Napoleon used his cavalry 'in a most surprising fashion.'[7] The main body of horse was formed in a vast, unmanoeuvrable block of three corps under Murat, and to begin with it was positioned opposite the Bagration Flèches and the northern flank of the Utitsa woods – obstacles which denied it a free run at the enemy. Later in the morning the cavalry performed well but hardly brilliantly in the battle against the Russian infantry and cavalry around Semenovskaya. Thereafter the weary horsemen had to carry out tasks which ought to have fallen to the infantry – holding the centre of the front for three hours under heavy fire, then storming into the Raevsky Redoubt. As for Napoleon's gunners, they managed to hold their own until shortly before the final artillery duel, despite the diversity and comparative lightness of their pieces.

The Russians fought in a strangely consistent style which did not necessarily owe much to the arrangements which had been worked out before the battle.

The Russian jaegers caved in under serious pressure rather more speedily than had been expected. They did notably badly in the morning at the village of Borodino and around the Raevsky Redoubt, and the only jaegers who really lived up to their reputation were those lurking in the neck of the woods between the Bagration Flèches and the Utitsa mound. With the collapse of the jaegers the brunt of the fighting was borne by the garrisons of the field fortifications, seconded by some enterprising counter-attacks by the battalion columns of heavy infantry. This, however, was a very costly way of fighting, for the dense columns offered perfect targets for the enemy artillery. Casualties were so heavy, and the gaps in the line were so wide, that the reserve had to be fed into the battle much earlier than had been anticipated. In later actions of the campaign, beginning with the affair of the rearguard at Mozhaisk, the Russians were careful to deploy the infantry in longer and thinner lines.

The Russian cavalry operated to deadly effect. On a roomier field of battle the light formation of individual corps and divisions might well have proved too flimsy to withstand the onslaught of the massive combined corps of the French, but here the Russian cavalry moved with assurance and speed, and repeatedly caught the Napoleonic horsemen off balance as they surged around an infantry square, a burnt-out village or a fortification.

The artillery in the Russian fortifications stuck to their guns to the last, as they had been told. Otherwise the handling of the artillery was profoundly unsatisfactory. Despite the overall superiority in number of guns the artillery managed to fire only 60,000 rounds, the same as the French, and for all the advantage of calibre of the Russian heavy ordnance we more than once encounter wretched batteries of horse artillery which were crushed by the weightier shot and shell of the French field guns.

The explanation lies in the irresponsibility of Kutaisov, who was more interested in involving himself in the hand-to-hand fighting than getting all his guns into action. For the sake of decency Kutuzov spoke of his regret at the young man's death, but Captain Golitsyn was watching the generalissimo's face and saw that his expression did not match his words. Golitsyn testifies that 'our ignorance of Kutaisov's arrangements for the artillery meant that on every sector of the battle-field we had fewer pieces in action than the French, and that in some places ordinary field artillery was pitted against the enemy battery guns. It is also worth mentioning that Kutuzov repeatedly said that, in his opinion, this deficiency accounted for our limited success.'[8]

As individuals the Russian army, corps and divisional commanders put up some oustanding performances. Occasionally, as in the recapture of the Raevsky Redoubt from Morand's division, a combined move of several units was effected by a number of aggressively-minded officers working together almost by accident, rather like the Union officers who defended Round Top on the second day at Gettysburg in 1863. The Russians would certainly have been lost without the dedication of Barclay, who had forged the army into a weapon fit to withstand Napoleon in the first place, and who overcame repeated crises on the right and centre of the position at Borodino.

Not the least of Barclay's tribulations was the peculiar state of affairs at Kutuzov's headquarters behind Gorki, a remote station from which staff officers occasionally rode forth with orders to move one unit or another about the field. Figuratively speaking Barclay was beating off the enemy with one hand and groping behind him with the other for reinforcements from the reserve; thanks to Kutusov's sporadic interventions there were at least two occasions when that hand closed on empty air.

It was fortunate that Colonel Toll was persuasive enough to gain Kutuzov's curt assent to the counterblow of the cavalry of Uvarov and Platov against the extreme left flank of the *Grande Armée*. Conceived so casually, and carried out with so little determination, this operation nevertheless paralysed Napoleon's army for two or more hours and gave Barclay the opportunity to rally his almost broken forces. As Captain Bolgovski categorically states, 'that manoeuvre of Platov's determined the fate of the Russian army'.[9] In its far-reaching moral effects the move is best compared with the 'hopeless' counter-attack of the seventy-four battered British tanks south of Arras on 21 May, 1940, which may well have saved the B.E.F. from destruction.

141

Kutuzov's inactivity is closely paralleled by the somnolence of Napoleon himself. Significantly the Emperor's most important decisions were largely negative ones – *not* to carry out Davout's project of the night march around the Russian position, *not* to throw in the Imperial Guard when the Russian centre appeared to have been broken.

The will of these two great leaders seems to have been paralysed by the weight of their responsibilities, a burden possibly heavier than that borne by any other commander in the nineteenth century. By any standard the scale of the forces engaged at Borodino was colossal, exceeding by a good third the size of the rival armies at Waterloo three years later. As for the intensity of the fighting, the Russians probably lost more men in a single span of eleven hours than any modern army before 1 July, 1916, the first day of the Battle of the Somme. By then, of course, commanders enjoyed the facilities of electrical communications. Indeed, if there is a good deal at Borodino to remind us of Gettysburg there is still more which anticipates the character of the 1914-1918 Western Front as a whole, with its mass conscript armies brought into conflict on a theatre with closed flanks.

When all this has been said, we are left with a lingering suspicion that the rival commanders might have been able to arrange affairs more conveniently than they did.

Kutuzov, decrepit and exhausted, was unwilling or unable to make use of the channels of communication and the system of staff support that Barclay had worked out in his *Yellow Book*. The scamperings and inspirations of a person like Colonel Toll were no substitute for the work of a body of trained and trusted staff officers.

Napoleon was in an even worse state, for he had never encouraged a sense of initiative among his subordinates. He tried to conduct Borodino as dictatorially as his earlier battles, forgetting that he was no longer the lithe young general of the 1790s. At Waterloo he was beaten by armies that were run on different lines: Wellington was every bit as autocratic as the Emperor in his habits of command, but thanks to his physical and mental activity he was able to ride to any point on the battlefield where his presence was needed, and he kept himself informed of the general course of the struggle through a veritable corps of young adjutants. His Prussian ally, Blücher, enjoyed the support of a staff very much like that which Barclay had trained in Russia; which was why the Prussian army displayed such an impressive continuity of direction in the days before Waterloo, even though Blücher was temporarily incapacitated by a fall from his horse.

In the normally accepted sense of the word the Russians clearly 'lost' the Battle of Borodino. They had suffered such heavy casualties that they could not possibly have renewed the fight, and they fell back along the Moscow road, abandoning the field to the French. Over the following days Kutuzov became convinced of the folly of any further attempt to keep the French out of the capital, and on 13 September he told his generals that he would withdraw the army and abandon the city to the enemy, 'for the loss of Moscow does not signify the loss of Russia, and I see my first duty as the preservation of the army.'[10]

And yet, with the advantage of hindsight, we may trace the ultimate destruction of Napoleon and his *Grande Armée* back to the hours of their greatest triumph, just after the capture of the Raevsky Redoubt. Now that the Emperor had advanced so far into Russia he would be content with nothing less than the destruction of the enemy's will to continue the war, yet each minute brought unwelcome evidence that the resolve of the Russians was as strong as ever.

The true victors of Borodino were the men who dragged the dead and wounded towards the green-coated officers rallying the Tsar's battalions in the fading light.

Chapter 10

AFTER THE BATTLE

The French were in no hurry to try conclusions again, so the weary Russians were allowed to trail east towards Moscow almost undisturbed. On 13 September, in a log hut at Fili, Kutuzov assembled his generals and debated whether the army should attempt to hold the capital or continue the retreat and recruit its forces for a counter-offensive. Bennigsen was all for making a stand, but Barclay, Tolstoy, Konovnitsyn, Raevsky and Toll were in favour of marching through Moscow and out the other side. Kutuzov agreed with the majority, and stated that 'by the very fact of abandoning Moscow we prepare the inevitable ruin of the enemy army'.[1]

Early on the morning of 14 September the French reached the hills to the west of Moscow and saw the gilded roofs and cupolas of the city rising from the middle of a fertile plain. A closer view would have shown them that the capital was by no means as tranquil as it seemed, for the streets were full of dusty soldiers and the civilian population was streaming towards the country on the orders of Rostopchin, the civilian governor. Military transport was intermingled with carts that were piled high with the goods and chattels of the refugees, and every breakdown produced a prodigious jam of vehicles and human beings.

Murat and the French advance guard reached the western gates while the Russian army was still trying to extricate itself from the tangle. However, General Miloradovich bought the necessary time by sending word to Murat that the French could have an unresisted entry to the city as long as they let the Russians file out undisturbed. During the negotiations Murat was surrounded by a swarm of fascinated cossacks. He gave his money and his watch to his admirers, and then ordered his entourage to hand over their watches as well.

At three in the afternoon Napoleon and the Imperial Guard arrived before the Dragomilov Gate. The Emperor had ex-

26 The Battle of Maloyaroslavets, from a lithograph in the
Historical Museum, Moscow. *(Novosti Press Agency)*

27 The Battle at Smolensk, from a lithograph in the
Historical Museum, Moscow. *(Novosti Press Agency)*

28 French troops in Smolensk, 28 October, 1812. *(Novosti Press Agency)*

29 Gallery of the War of 1812 in the Hermitage, Leningrad. Each panel contains
a portrait of one of the Russian commanders. *(Novosti Press Agency)*

pected to be met by a deputation of the city elders, bearing the municipal keys and other tokens of submission. Instead he rode in through an untended gate, and the boots and hooves of the *Grand Armée* echoed through streets deserted save for a few convicts and wounded soldiers.

On the same evening a fire broke out in the bazaar quarter. The blaze was fanned by a strong wind and the flames raged unchecked until they were quenched by a rainstorm on 20 September. The Kremlin and about a quarter of the city nevertheless escaped undamaged, and Napoleon still had ample space to accommodate his 95,000 remaining troops in some comfort.

If the fire had been more devastating, or if the autumn weather had been worse, Napoleon might have begun his with-drawal there and then and saved the *Grande Armée* from its final ruin. As it was, he hung on in Moscow and sent out over-tures for terms of peace. Now that he had defeated the Russians and occupied their capital, he was sure that they would act like reasonable Europeans and meet his demands. He wrote first to Alexander on 20 September, putting the blame for the burning of Moscow on Rostopchin, and suggesting that even now he might be prepared to accept some accommoda-tion: 'If Your Majesty still conserves for me some remnant of your former feelings, you will take this letter in good part.'

There was no reply, and so at the beginning of October Napoleon sent Count Lauriston (his former Ambassador to St Petersburg) to Kutuzov to negotiate an armistice and open up another path of communication. Kutuzov received the emissary with caution and declared that he had no power to negotiate the truce. Even so Alexander was furious when he heard of the talks, and re-affirmed that he was totally inflexible in pursuit of his sacred duty to avenge the injuries of his country.

While Napoleon waited for a word from the Tsar his lethargy grew worse and he spent long periods rummaging through the boxes of his travelling library. His favourite reading at this time was a little volume of Voltaire's *History of Charles XII*, which suggests a number of interesting comparisons between his own adventure and the ill-fated Swedish invasion of Russia in 1708.

Every now and then the French troops were made painfully aware that they were standing at the end of a salient driven 550 miles into hostile territory. The cossacks managed to interrupt the communications near Mazhaisk on 24 September, and a party of chasseurs and dragoons of the Imperial Guard were wiped out when they tried to re-open the road a little later.

Even this sobering episode failed to dampen the jollifications for long, and the breakdown of the *Grande Armée*'s discipline continued unabated. The German bandmaster Klinkhardt reached Moscow while the merrymaking was in full swing and came across 'a scene of confusion such as I have never seen before. On one side I saw a soldier spinning tall stories to a circle of attentive hearers, while nearby other men were settling an affair of honour by a duel. At one moment the street rang with the music of a military band, and the next with the chatter of officers who were strolling arm in arm. We could see happy faces beaming through the palace windows, and there were even some pretty ladies who honoured us with a nod. Everything was full of movement and life. We saw nothing of the horrors of war till we reached the foot of the Kremlin, where another kind of view stretched before us: the long wide streets had been turned into heaps of charred ruins, and wherever we walked there was nothing to be seen except smouldering débris, which flared into bright flame with every puff of wind.'[2]

During the whole period of their retreat from Moscow the Rusian soldiers could see the distant flames of the burning capital, and every now and then the wind would blow ashes over their heads. 'The Russians had learnt to accept the fiery sacrifice of Smolensk and many other towns with a certain degree of resignation, but now the burning-down of Moscow filled them all with deep sadness and intensified their anger against the enemy.'[3]

As if sensing the general change of mood, Kutuzov moved the army off the Ryazan road, which ran to the south-east, and directed it to a position twenty-five miles due south of Moscow behind the River Pakhra. It was not until 26 September that Murat was able to find out exactly where the Russians had gone. Kutuzov thereupon decamped and retreated to a

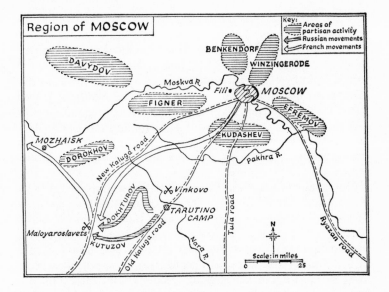

Region of MOSCOW

Key:
Areas of partisan activity
Russian movements
French movements

BENKENDORF
WINZINGERODE
DAVYDOV
Moskva R.
Fili• MOSCOW
FIGNER
EFREMOV
MOZHAISK
DOROKHOV
New Kaluga road
KUDASHEV
Pakhra R.
DOKHTUROV
×Vinkovo
TARUTINO CAMP
Tula road
Maloyaroslavets
KUTUZOV
Old Kaluga road
Nara R.
Ryazan road
N
Scale: in miles
0   25

second position at Tarutino, behind the steep banks of the River Nara. He reported with satisfaction that 'the enemy have lost our army from view, and in their bewilderment they are sending strong detachments in all directions to discover where we are.'[4] Murat did not come up with the Russians again until 4 October. He saw that their position was manifestly too strong to be attacked, and he drew the advance guard back to his camp at Vinkovo.

The camp at Tarutino was nicely chosen to block the Tula and Kaluga roads and Kutuzov wrote that it conserved for him 'all the resources which have been prepared in our most fertile districts. A retreat in any other direction would have denied these riches to me, and it would have cut my contact with the armies of Tormasov and Chichagov.'[5] Among the 'resources' which Kutuzov had in mind were the agricultural produce of the fertile south and the weapons produced by the Tula arms factory and the Bryansk gun foundry. Every day spent in the Tarutino camp Kutuzov considered 'golden', for it marked a notable increase in the strength of his army and a progressive diminution in the fighting capabilities of the French.

147

When the Russian army entered the Tarutino camp it numbered 85,000 weary men. Recruits poured in by the thousands over the next three weeks, and the peasants and sutlers brought in wine, vodka, grapes and melons, which they sold to the troops. Kutuzov was to resume the campaign with an army 120,000 strong, restored in morale as well as numbers. It was particularly significant that the 10,000 Russian regular cavalry and the 20,000 cossacks enjoyed a convincing superiority over the horse of the *Grande Armée*, which was nominally 14,500 strong but now had only about 4,600 cavalry really fit for service.

During the retreat from Borodino the First and Second West Armies had become inextricably intermingled, and Kutuzov therefore took the opportunity to unite them in a single body. Barclay felt that he had become the fifth wheel on the coach, and he bade good-bye to the army on 4 October on the excuse of bad health. His inveterate enemy Ermolov put on a great show of emotion in the Russian fashion, embracing him in a bear-like hug and bursting into tears. Bennigsen, that bird of ill-omen, was replaced as chief-of-staff by the capable Konovnitsyn. The heroic Bagration was soon out of the running altogether. The wound in his leg failed to heal and he died of a general infection on 24 September.

The war was fast becoming an affair of nations, and not just troops and generals, and Kutuzov soon had very considerable popular forces to throw into the scale. By the end of the year 192,000 volunteers had signed up with the *opolchenie*, which had been transformed from a serf militia into one of the principal expressions of national enthusiasm. They were organized into units of jaegers and mounted and foot 'cossacks', and were put to a variety of useful tasks: some helped to fill out the lines of battle of the main army, while others assisted in the blockade of Moscow or occupied towns and roads along the possible routes of enemy escape.

In areas subject to enemy occupation the resistance took a still more direct form, in the shape of a widespread and, at first, mostly spontaneous guerrilla movement. This phenomenon fitted in very well with Kutuzov's initial strategy, which was 'to avoid general actions while waging a war of raids and outposts'.[6] He was quick to appreciate the potentialities of his

148

hairy allies and told Denis Davydov that 'it does not matter to me that these people wear caps rather than military shakos, or that they are clad in peasant smocks instead of proper uniforms'.[7]

Kutuzov reinforced and directed the peasant partisans with enterprising commanders who led 'flying columns' of jaegers, dragoons, hussars, cossacks and light artillery. The French communications between Moscow and Smolensk were plagued by the bands of General Dorokhov, Colonel Vadbolsky and Lieutenant-Colonel Denis Davydov, while Colonels Kudashev and Efremov were active on the other roads leading out of Moscow.

This was an exceptionally demanding kind of warfare and many lessons had to be learned the hard way. After one of Dorokhov's units had been trapped by the enemy, Kutuzov wrote that the flying columns 'should rest in one place only as long as is necessary to feed the men and horses. Their marches should be secretive and directed along minor roads. Whenever they come to some kind of habitation they must be careful to let no-one wander off, lest news of their presence should reach the enemy. In daylight they should hide up in woods or broken ground. To sum up, the flying columns must be decisive, swift and tireless.'[8]

As for the ways of inflicting damage on the enemy, Kutuzov advised one of the commanders who was working west of Moscow that 'the chief objectives of your operations should be to attack the small enemy detachments and transports proceeding along the Smolensk road, and to destroy the enemy magazines established along the same route. At the same time you ought to burn the fodder in the villages of that region, and take away anything else which might facilitate the supply of the enemy cavalry and artillery. In particular you should do everything you can to intercept the French couriers and bring them immediately to headquarters.'[9]

On 12 September Colonel Chernyshev set out from St Petersburg for the army with Alexander's plan of campaign. The Tsar (or rather his entourage) envisaged a complicated working-together of the three Russian armies to bring about the ruin of the enemy. Kutuzov, with the main force was to follow the *Grande Armée* to encourage it on its way westwards, while the decisive rôle was given to the two forces massing on either side of the path back to Poland. General Wittgenstein's force (see p. 51) was to csmbine with General Stein heil's 10,000 troops from Finland and march south to make contact with the other jaw of the strategic pincers, which was to consist of the united forces of Admiral Chichagov's Army of the Danube and the Third West Army (Tormasov). All the forces were to join up in the region of the western Russian watershed near Borisov, where the nearly continuguous river lines of the Ulla and the Berezina restricted the channel of the *Grande Armée*'s escape (see Map 13, p. 156).

The strategy alloted Kutuzov's army an excessively passive part in the combined operation, and it had been drawn up under the mistaken impression that the French had been worsted at Borodino. All the same Kutuzov was willing to embrace the scheme, with a few minor reservations, and the broad principles guided Russian operations until the end of November.

At Tarutino a new offensive spirit gripped all ranks of the main Russian army, and Colonel Toll worked out a plan for dealing a blow at the French advance guard which was resting nearby at Vinkovo. Toll won over Konovnitsyn and Baggovut, and the generals persuaded a highly unwilling Kutuzov to sanction the attack. The detailed plans were drawn up on 16 October, in preparation for the operation on the next day, but General Ermolov went off to a private dinner party and the requisite orders failed to reach the regiments. Kutuzov was in ignorance of what had happened, and when he toured the camp the following day he was astounded to find the army taking its ease. His anger was focussed on a shabbily-dressed man who was riding by on a fat little horse, and he yelled out to him: 'What kind of scum are you?' The reply came back: 'Captain of the general staff Brosin, quartermaster of the I Cavalry Corps.'[10] Kutuzov continued on his way somewhat abashed.

The attack was finally launched early on the 18th. The Russians could scarcely have found a more suitable target, for Murat's cavalry were still stunned after their ordeal at Borodino and the troopers were regaining their shattered wits amid a beautiful landscape of oak woods and fields of standing corn. The new commander of I Cavalry Corps, General Sébastiani, assumed, like most people, that hostilities were practically at an end, and he slopped around in his slippers clutching a volume of Italian verse. Thus he achieved the unwelcome distinction of being caught off his guard by an enemy army twice in the same campaign (see p. 60): one might have thought that the resemblance of the names Inkovo and Vinkovo would have stirred some alarm bells in his mind.

A Prussian officer in the 1st Light Cavalry recalls that the horses were being fed at daybreak when suddenly 'the air was filled with a shrill cossack cry. We threw ourselves on our horses, while the rest of the division rode out of the encampment against the enemy. The plain was swarming everywhere with cossacks, and regular cavalry and artillery were following them at the trot. On the left they had already burst through the Poles and they were threatening our flank from that direction. Being so badly mounted, all the cavalry of our field watch had been killed or wounded; only the infantry were left to withdraw in tight formations over the plain, surrounded by thick masses of cossacks who kept up a terrible yell and did everything they could to hinder their retreat. Sometimes our troops disappeared in the throng altogether, but every time that they halted and gave a volley the cossacks disappeared in all directions, which enabled our men to resume their speedy retreat. Thus they finally reached the defile of Vinkovo in the best of order.'[11]

The whole of the French advance guard might have been overrun if the co-ordination of the refurbished Russian army had been as admirable as its enthusiasm. The units had not had enough time to shake themselves down, and they were hardly up to carrying out the plan of attack, which was an over-elaborate affair of five columns. The heroic Baggovut was killed by a cannon shot, which increased the confusion, and to the fury of the officers Kutuzov held back the left wing so far behind the rest that it took hardly any part in the action. All the same Murat's command was badly mauled, suffering 2,500 casualties and losing 2,000 prisoners and 38 of its 187 guns before it made good its escape.

Meanwhile Napoleon had decided that there was no point in hanging on in the increasingly isolated city of Moscow while the Russians were still unwilling to listen to terms. He proposed instead to take the *Grande Armée* on a wide circuit south and west through a tract of fertile and untouched countryside to the area of Minsk-Mohilev-Smolensk-Vitebsk, where he would establish winter quarters and prepare a base for a campaign against St Petersburg in 1813. He drew up his plans on 16 October, intending to begin the evacuation of Moscow on the 20th. However, on hearing of the encounter at Vinkovo, he brought the date forward by a day, and the first troops left the city on the 19th, with Eugène and the Royal Italian Guard in the lead. Altogether 95,000 men filed out of the city, laden down with useless booty of all kinds, and encumbered with swarms of camp-followers, five hundred guns and thousands of vehicles. Marshal Mortier and the rearguard departed last of all, after they had fired a number of demolition mines in the Kremlin on the 23rd.

On the night of 22/23 October the hussar officer Akinfov was ordered to carry the news of the evacuation to Kutuzov. '. . . the night was cold and the moon was shining in the sky. I left my companions behind me, because I had an excellent horse, and after a remarkably quick journey I arrived at headquarters and galloped straight to the quarters of General Konovnitsyn, whom I found seated at a table at work. He was astonished by my news and at once called Colonel Toll. They took my report and went to rouse the field-marshal, leaving me at the entrance of his log cabin. He summoned me immediately: he was still on his bed, though he was clad in his tunic and was wearing his decorations. His presence was majestic but his eyes were dancing with joy. "Well, me friend," he said, "has Napoleon really left Moscow? Tell me quickly: don't leave me waiting." I made a detailed report, and when I had finished this venerable old man turned towards the icon of our Saviour and spoke aloud: "God, my Creator, thou hast finally heard my prayers. Henceforth Russia is delivered!" '[12]

From Moscow Napoleon first struck south along the Old Kaluga Road, then veered west by secondary roads intending to slip around Kutuzov's left flank to the important road junction at Maloyaroslavets, from where a variety of routes would take him through untouched country to Smolensk.

Kutozov sent General Dokhturov ahead with VI Corps and

I Cavalry Corps to intercept Eugène and his Italians, in the belief that they were merely an unsupported detachment of foragers. Dokhturov and Eugène marched neck and neck along converging routes through the night of 23/24 September and reached Maloyaroslavets almost together at five in the morning, which led to a bloody eighteen-hour encounter-battle for the possession of the blazing town. Kutuzov now divined Napoleon's strategy, and assembled his main army a mile to the south of Maloyaroslavets, resolved to give battle on the next day rather than let the French break through to Kaluga. As he told an enemy officer afterwards, he stood his ground 'because it was essential for me to force you to go back along the route which you had earlier devastated yourselves'.[13]

None of this was of much comfort to Dokhturov, who was left to fight at Maloyaroslavets throughout the 24th with no help from the main army except Raevsky's VII Corps. This reinforcement was soon swallowed up, and when Eugène put in his last division (General Pino's) the balance finally swung in favour of the Italians and they drove the Russians from the town. Five or six thousand men were lost on each side.

In the evening Napoleon repaired to the nearby village of Grodnia to consider whether it was still possible for him to effect a breakthrough. He entered a peasant cabin, where he had a map spread out on the table and pondered, head in hands, for a full hour, watched by his silent staff. He had 63,000 troops immediately available, against perhaps more than 90,000 Russians, but he finally decided to take the risk and issued the outline orders for a battle on the following day. Murat, Bessières and General Lobau were deeply disturbed, for they held that even a 'victory' might prove ruinous to the enfeebled *Grande Armée*.

Napoleon rode out on the 25th to reconnoitre the Russian position. On the road to the town the Emperor and his staff drew some way ahead of their escort, though they were aware of the comforting presence of what seemed to be a troop of Polish lancers riding on a parallel course to their right. Suddenly the 'lancers' wheeled in on the road and scattered the glittering suite with an unmistakable cossack yell. The Saxon major von Burkersroda was in a force of cavalry which was sent to the rescue, and he recalls that 'as we rode up the side

153

of a hill the Emperor and his headquarters came streaming towards us in obvious confusion. Some officers had lost their hats, others seemed to be wounded and several horses were running around with empty saddles . . . We spurred our horses across the road as hard as we could, but the cossacks had disappeared in the mist.'[14]

Shortly afterwards Napoleon cancelled the orders for the battle, and on 26 October ordered the *Grande Armée* to break contact and head north to the main Smolensk road – the path along which it had advanced to Moscow. Perhaps he reached this momentous decision because he was deterred by what he had seen of Kutuzov's position; perhaps he had been alarmed by the news that the advanced guard of Poniatowski's corps had been destroyed in an action at Medyn on the 24th; or perhaps quite simply his nerve had been broken by his own narrow escape from the cossacks.

The *Grande Armée* reached the Smolensk road at Mozhaisk, then turned west through an all-too-familiar landscape. On the 29th the French crossed the field of Borodino, and Labaume records the hideous sight of a 'multitude of dead bodies, which deprived of burial fifty-two days, scarcely retained the human form. As we traversed the fields of Borodino, my consternation was inexpressible, when I found the forty thousand [sic] men, who had perished there, yet lying exposed. The whole plain was entirely covered with them. None of the bodies were more than half buried. In one place were to be seen garments still red with blood, and bones gnawed by dogs and birds of prey: in another were broken arms, drums, helmets and swords. On one side we saw the remains of the cottage at which Kutuzov had encamped, and more to the left, the famous redoubt. It still frowned threateningly over the plain. It rose like a pyramid in the middle of a desert.'[15]

The late autumn weather remained remarkably fine, though the first night frost was experienced at Gzhatsk. The discipline of the *Grande Armée,* already loosened by the stay in Moscow, now began to go to pieces under the strain of the march. While the cossacks and the peasant guerrillas grew bolder, flocks of crows began to gather in the brilliant blue sky, scenting feasts to come.

It did not occur to Kutuzov that the French would have

given up their objective so easily. He was sure that they were still bent on turning his left flank, and he therefore resumed the march on Kaluga on 27 October. Thus Russia witnessed the peculiar spectacle of two hostile armies hurrying away from each other on divergent courses. Kutuzov heard about the *Grande Armée*'s change of direction on the 28th, and only then did he appreciate the extent of his strategic victory. As he reported to Alexander, the brush on the 24th now proved to be 'one of the most significant days of this bloody war, for the action at Maloyaroslavets has had the fatal effect for the enemy of barring their path through the most fertile of our corn-growing provinces.'[16] If the Battle of Borodino showed that Napoleon could not defeat the Russians, then the encounter at Maloyaroslavets ensured not just that he was going to lose the war, but that his loss was going to be catastrophic

Kutuzov's subsequent strategy was destructive but unheroic. Certainly he stated that 'the one and only aim of all our operations is to do everything we possibly can to annihilate the enemy',[17] but at the same time he claimed that he could do the French most harm 'by moving along a parallel route',[18] in other words interposing his army between Napoleon and the untouched lands to the south of the main road. All the while the flying columns and bands of peasants were to cut down the enemy stragglers and foragers, and restrict the area from which Napoleon could draw his supplies. It was a kind of warfare that had been entirely familiar to soldiers in the middle of the eighteenth century: by such techniques the Austrians had turned Frederick the Great out of Bohemia in 1744, and ejected the French and Spanish from Lombardy two years later. By 1812, however, not all officers were capable of grasping the antique subtleties of Kutuzov's scheme, and people like Sir Robert Wilson were scandalized by the apparent callousness of the generalissimo in holding back the main army while the brunt of the fighting was borne by the advance guard.

Turning north, then west, in pursuit of the *Grande Armée*, Kutuzov sent ahead Platov's cossacks and two corps of infantry and two of cavalry under General Miloradovich. At ten in the morning of 3 November Miloradovich and Platov cut off Marshal Davout's I Corps near Vyazma. Eugène,

155

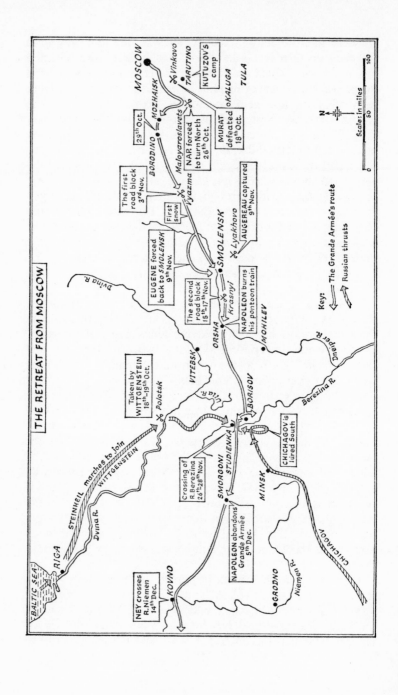

THE RETREAT FROM MOSCOW

MOSCOW

Vinkovo
TARUTINO

KUTUZOV'S camp

TULA

MOZHAISK
29th Oct.
BORODINO

Maloyaroslavets
NAP forced to turn North 26th Oct.

oKALUGA

MURAT defeated 18th Oct.

The first road block 3rd Nov.

Vyazma

First snow

AUGEREAU captured 9th Nov.

SMOLENSK

EUGENE forced back to SMOLENSK 9th Nov.

Lyakhovo

The second road block 15th–17th Nov.

Krasnyi

NAPOLEON burns his pontoon train

ORSHA

MOHILEV

Dvina R.

VITEBSK

Taken by WITTGENSTEIN 18th–19th Oct.

Polotsk

BORISOV

Berezina R.

Dnieper R.

Scale: in miles

N

0   50   100

STEINHEIL marches to join WITTGENSTEIN

WITTGENSTEIN

Ula R.

STUDIENKA

Crossing of R. Berezina 26th–28th Nov.

SMORGONI

CHICHAGOV is lured South

MINSK

Dvina R.

RIGA

BALTIC SEA

Niemen R.

KOVNO

NAPOLEON abandons Grande Armée 5th Dec.

NEY crosses R. Niemen 14th Dec.

GRODNO

Niemen R.

CHICHAGOV

Key:

The Grande Armée's route

Russian thrusts

Poniatowski and Ney turned back to help their comrade, and they dragged him free at a cost of 6,000 casualties and 2,500 prisoners. More significant than the size of the butcher's bill was the fact that the notoriously severely-disciplined I Corps streamed out of the trap in almost total disarray; if these troops could break there was not much hope for the cohesion of the rest of the *Grande Armée*. The French continued their retreat through the following night, every now and then 'startled by the report of cannon, which, passing over the thick forests, sounded in a mournful and horrible manner. The unexpected sound, repeated by the echoes of the valley, was lengthened into dismal reverberations'.[19]

Two days later the sky was suddenly obscured by a yellowish-grey overcast, and almost immediately the first snow of the winter descended in thick flakes, breaking down the branches of the fir trees and merging the landscape and the sky in an unbroken whiteness.

By now the more distant Russian armies were closing upon the *Grand Armée*'s path of retreat. Admiral Chichagov had left Osten-Sacken to hold down Schwarzenberg's Austrians and he was now erupting from the south with thirty thousand men. Wittgenstein and Steinheil simultaneously advanced from the other side and wrested the important staging post of Polotsk from the II and IV French Corps in a two-day battle on 18-19 October.

The bad news about Chichagov and Wittgenstein reached Napoleon at the beginning of November, and he had to give up all hope of consolidating the *Grande Armée* for the winter around Smolensk. Even the precious stores at Smolensk mostly went to waste, for the Imperial Guard and the other leading troops gobbled up and scattered the supplies in three days of looting which left the rearguard with nothing at all. Napoleon directed Eugène's corps north-east towards the depôt at Vitebsk, with the intention of easing the scrum around Smolensk, but before the Italians reached their destination they were caught on 9 November by Platov on the fords of the Vop. The survivors were left with no alternative but to make for Smolensk. On the same day the flying columns of Seslavin and Figner captured Augereau's brigade of two

157

thousand men at Lyakhovo on the road between Elnia and Smolensk. Kutuzov believed that this episode was peculiarly significant, for it was the first time in the war that an entire enemy unit had allowed itself to be taken prisoner.

Thus encouraged, Kutuzov went on to issue a ferocious general order on 10 November: 'After such extraordinary successes,' he wrote, 'what we have to do is to pursue the enemy as swiftly as we can. Then, perhaps, the French will leave their bones strewn over the soil of Russia – the same land which they intended to enslave . . . let us all remember the example of Suvorov: he knew how to put up with hunger and cold when the victory and glory of the Russian nation were at stake.'[20]

The first columns of the *Grande Armée* trailed out of Smolensk on 12 November. The corps were more than usually strung out, and Miloradovich practically cut the army in two parts on the 15th, when he came up from the south with his 16,000-strong command and placed himself across the main road near Krasnyi. Napoleon and the Imperial Guard had already passed through in safety, but the corps of Eugène, Davout and Ney were stranded on the wrong side of the roadblock. On the 16th Eugène fought his way through to Napoleon with three thousand of his original force of five thousand. The other corps were still trapped, and so on the 17th Napoleon and the Imperial Guard barged their way through the roadblock and back again, thus enabling Davout to make good his escape. Ney had disappeared altogether among the Russian hordes. The Emperor was astonished and delighted when 'the bravest of the brave' worked his own salvation and turned up with one thousand survivors at Orsha on the 21st.

The dire emergency at Krasnyi seems to have inspired Napoleon with some of the brilliance he had shown in his younger days. Kutuzov, however, was terrified of meeting Napoleon face to face on a new battlefield, and he was careful to withhold the main Russian army from the combat. His own officers were embarrassed by the obvious anxiety he had shown when he tried to find out from prisoners whether the Emperor was present in person. All the same the harrowing days at Krasnyi cost the *Grande Armée* 6,000 dead and wounded and about 20,000 prisoners. The artillery lost 116 guns and the cavalry practically ceased to exist.

Already on 1 November Platov had reported that the French army was fleeing 'in a manner in which no other army has ever fled in history, casting aside all its baggage, sick and wounded'.[21] Just over a week later Berthier told the Emperor that hardly any regiment retained more than one quarter of its men with the colours, the rest having wandered off to forage for themselves or escape the bounds of discipline.

The tens of thousands of stragglers were almost defenceless, and the woods were ringing with the cries of the vengeful peasants. Wilson came across one group of *muzhiks* who were beating out the brains of a line of prisoners to the time of a song. He heard how at another place 'a detachment of fifty of the enemy had been surprised. The peasants resolved to bury them alive in a pit: a drummer boy bravely led the devoted party and sprang into the grave. A dog belonging to one of the victims could not be secured; every day, however, the dog went into the neighbouring camp, and came back with a bit of food in his mouth to sit and moan over the newly-turned earth.'[22]

In the last week of November the surviving armies of the Russian and Napoleonic empires converged on the River Berezina. Chichagov's 30,000 men were ready to interlock with the 25,000 of Wittgenstein, while Kutuzov with 80,000 was pushing the *Grande Armée* into the closing trap. The weather had played Napoleon a cruel trick. A week earlier the winter had seemed to be set in so firmly that he burnt his pontoon train at Orsha, confident that he would be able to cross the frozen rivers dryshod. Now an unseasonable thaw had turned the ice into drifting mush, and the *Grande Armée* was marooned on the east bank of the Berezina.

Napoleon ranged up and down the river line like a trapped fox. The slow-witted Chichagov on the far bank was cast in the unlikely rôle of a hunter, and he allowed himself to be lured downstream by a demonstration which Napoleon arranged for his benefit to the south of Borisov. Meanwhile General Eblé and the French sappers were immersed to their necks in the icy waters building two bridges upstream at Studianka, to the north of Borisov. The crossing began on 26

November and was still in progress two days later when the Russians reappeared in force. Chichagov advanced up the west bank with notable slowness and was checked short of the bridgehead by a violent fire-fight in the woods.

Wittgenstein had better luck on the east bank. He captured the 4,500 troops of General Parthonneaux's division, which had walked into him by accident, and he proceeded to plant his guns within range of the bridges. The near bank was still crowded with some 30,000 stragglers, and just as they were about to rush the bridges the shot from Wittgenstein's artillery 'rained down in the midst of them. The enormous mass of men, horses and carts piled up at the entrances to the bridges and jammed together in an insurmountable obstacle . . . Very many men, unable to reach the entries, were pushed by the crowd into the Berezina where they nearly all drowned.

'To add to the horror one of the bridges collapsed under the weight of the guns and the heavy caissons which followed them. Everyone flocked towards the other bridge, where the disorder was already so great that even some of the strongest men were overcome by the pressure and suffocated. Seeing that it was impossible to cross the jammed bridges, many drivers urged their horses into the river . . . but the result was that the waggons collided and overturned. A few vehicles managed to reach the far bank. Unfortunately the general staff had made no arrangements to grade the banks, which would have made the ascent easier, and so very few of the carts managed to climb the slope. Thus another multitude of people were drowned.'[23]

When Kutuzov's troops arrived on the scene they found that 'for a distance of one thousand yards around the two enemy bridges the ground and the river were so obstructed with the bodies of men and horses that at some points it was possible to cross the Berezina on foot.'[24] All told Napoleon crossed the Berezina at the cost of several thousand men who were killed or wounded in the fighting, and about twenty thousand more who were stranded and captured on the east bank.

Napoleon continued his march with 'twenty thousand disarmed soldiers, without linen, and without stockings, whose only shoes were manufactured from their worn-out hats, and

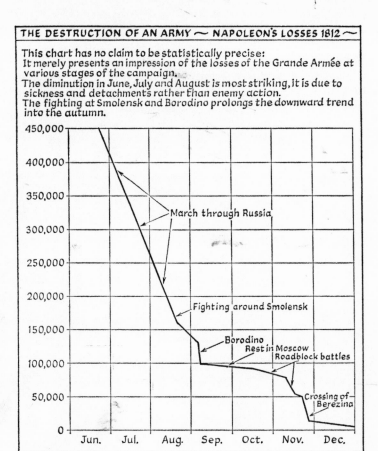

THE DESTRUCTION OF AN ARMY ～ NAPOLEON'S LOSSES 1812 ～

This chart has no claim to be statistically precise:
It merely presents an impression of the losses of the Grande Armée at various stages of the campaign.
The diminution in June, July and August is most striking, it is due to sickness and detachments rather than enemy action.
The fighting at Smolensk and Borodino prolongs the downward trend into the autumn.

450,000
400,000
350,000
300,000
250,000
200,000
150,000
100,000
50,000
0

Jun.   Jul.   Aug.   Sep.   Oct.   Nov.   Dec.

March through Russia

Fighting around Smolensk

Borodino
Rest in Moscow
Roadblock battles

Crossing of Berezina

whose shoulders were covered with pieces of sacking, and the skins of horses, newly flayed.'[25] Not just the campaign but the army was lost beyond all hope of retrieval, and on 5 December Napoleon left the command in the hands of Murat and sped on by sledge towards the Polish frontier. The abandoned 'army' straggled back through Vilna, losing men every hour to the fury of the winter and the cossacks. On 14 December Marshal Ney led the 'rearguard' over the frontier at Kovno, and the campaign of 1812 was effectively at an end. Of the 450,000-strong central group of the *Grande Armée* which had

161

set out six months before, just one thousand effective combatants and a few thousand stragglers survived to re-cross the Niemen.

Kutuzov was only reporting the literal truth when he wrote to Tsar Alexander on 22 December that 'the war has finished with the complete destruction of the enemy'.[26]

Chapter 11

BORODINO IN HISTORY AND FICTION

The first Russian studies of Borodino and the War of 1812 were veritable 'literary monuments', erected by officers who had taken part in the events they described and were anxious to construct narratives that were at once factually complete and suitably flattering to the Russian high command and the person of the Tsar. D. I. Akhsharumov's history of 1819[1] held the field until the appearance of the massive works of Colonel D. P. Buturlin[2] and Lieutenant-General A. I. Mikhailovsky-Danilevsky[3] in the late 1820's and the 1830's. Both were 'official' historians who could refresh their memories from secret documents and whose works were subsidised from public funds. Mikhailovsky-Danilevsky was particularly well-placed to write an authoritative account, for he had acted as one of Kutuzov's adjutants in the campaigns of 1812 and 1813 and had been wounded at Vinkovo. It was unfortunate that he attributed all the important decisions of strategy to Tsar Alexander, and left all questions of interpretation to 'the military pedagogues who teach strategy and tactics'.[4] This was a reference to his bitter personal enemy M. I. Bogdanovich (1805-1882), a young instructor at the Staff College. The broadside did not, however, prevent Bogdanovich from stepping into Mikhailovsky-Danilevsky's shoes as the official Court historian of the middle decades of the nineteenth century. Indeed Bogdanovich's own account (1859-60)[5] was compiled from a greater variety of sources than the earlier histories and was distinguished by the genuine attempt to assess the morale of the armies and the characters of the various commanders.

It was therefore against a background of widening historical appreciation that Russia fêted the half-century of the War of 1812. Monuments began to sprout on the salient points of the battlefield of Borodino, and in 1867 Tolstoy visited an already

163

well-marked site when he was gathering material for his epic novel *War and Peace.*

The approach of the centenary galvanized scores of scholars into activity. The Russian General Staff was quick off the mark, and in 1900 its historians published the first of twenty-four volumes of relevant documents[6]. The centenary year itself was marked by the appearance of two monographs on the Battle of Borodino[7], and a collective study of the impact of the War on Russian society.[8] The fortifications on the field of Borodino were elaborately restored, though the first excavation of the ditches revealed such a mass of bones that the renovated ditches had to be set about ten yards to the rear.

The October Revolution of 1917 accomplished a complete break in the tradition of Russian military scholarship, and the first dozen years of Soviet rule produced no studies of the War of 1812 except for a few pamphlets which were issued for internal consumption in the military schools. The founding of the *Voenno-Istorichesky Zhurnal* in 1931 marked the beginning of a revival of interest, though it was scarcely permissable to write with any enthusiasm about any aspect of Tsarist military history until 1941, when the Germans invaded Russia and Stalin saw that he must conjure heroic figures out of the past to foster national feeling. The grey creed of Communism was not enough in itself to stir people's imaginations. E. V. Tarle and other historians promptly published a collection of documents on the Napoleonic adventure of 1812[9] with 'the aim of popularising one of the most brilliant pages of Russian military history in terms that would broaden the struggle of the Soviet people against the German Fascists.'[10] The work of familiarising the people with the better traditions of the past was shared by B. B. Kafengauz[11] and N. Korobkov[12] who praised Suvorov in terms so unmeasured as to embarrass later Soviet historians, who had to point out that the Tsarist army was, after all, the upholder of a vicious class system.

The last few years of Stalin's rule witnessed the publication of some useful collections of biographical documents under the general title of *Russkie Polkovodtsy,* most notably the volumes devoted to Kutuzov and Bagration.[13] A bibliographer commented in 1969 that 'the bringing of these collections of documents and materials to the light of day may be largely explained by reference to the circumstances of the Great Patriotic War of 1941-45, where the names of Suvorov, Kutuzov, Ushakov and Nakhimov helped to make our progressive military traditions better known.'[14]

The heroic 'personality cult' culminated in 1955 with the appearance of *Polkovodets Kutuzov,* a collection of articles published under the editorship of L. G. Beskrovny, the doyen of Russian military historians in the 1950's and 1960's. The general tone may be assessed from the assertion that 'the triumph of Kutuzov's strategy and tactics in the struggle with Napoleon represented a victory of the Russian school of warfare. As the heir and successor of the glorious Suvorov, Kutuzov developed the lessons contained in his book *The Art of Victory* and deepened and widened the warlike skill of the Russian nation.'[15]

In all of this the historians were still following the lead which had been given by Stalin in 1947, when he tried to explain away the débâcle of 1941 by claiming that he had been putting into effect the methods of Kutuzov, a military genius who deliberately lured the French into the depths of the country before he launched a devastating counter-offensive.

In later years Beskrovny and other historians adopted a more thematic approach to the War of 1812. The rôle of the *opolchenie* was stressed in a further collection of documents,[16] though B.S. Abalikhin tried to show that, far from alleviating the class struggle, the war strengthened the peasants' resolve to free themselves from serfdom. The 150th anniversary of the struggle saw the publication of a detailed survey and bibliography by Beskrovny,[17] and the invaluable *Borodino, Dokumenty,*[18] a wide and representative selection of reports and memoirs relating to the battle.

In 1968 one of Beskrovny's pupils, General P. A. Zhilin, testified to the abiding interest in the war by publishing his comprehensive history *The Destruction of Napoleon's Army in Russia*[19]. Zhilin gave vent to strident denunciations of bourgeois historians, and drew the attention of his readers to the modern relevance of the study of the War of 1812: 'During its long history international Imperialism has acquired considerable experience of piratical wars. It is therefore essential

165

for us to know how aggressive enterprises were hatched against our land, and to study how we received the invaders. Thus we may unmask the contemporary revanchists and aggressors, and thwart them before they can unleash new wars. These questions are not only of interest in themselves, but they are laden with considerable theoretical and practical significance. The student ignores them at his peril, for here we see how closely history is linked with modern times.'[20]

If one disregards his more ferocious passages, Zhilin presents a reasonably balanced survey of the war from the Russian point of view. The treatment of Borodino is eminently fair. While showing that Kutuzov planned to fight and was not in any sense 'forced' into the battle, Zhilin denies that the battle was a turning point in the war, and shows that the Russians sustained unnecessarily heavy casualties on account of their deep tactical formations: earlier historians had been inclined to argue that Borodino somehow represented a decisive Russian 'victory', and that the suicidal mass formation was an admirable way of fighting battles.

Zhilin also takes issue with his predecessors over the rôle of 'natural factors' in the destruction of Napoleon's troops. He accuses E. V. Tarle[21] and M. Pokrovsky[22] of exaggerating the impact of climate and terrain, and thereby presenting an all too passive view of the work of the Russian army, which, in Zhilin's opinion, far from having prepared a 'golden bridge' for the French, actively hounded them to their doom.

All the same Zhilin fails to provide concrete evidence to refute Wilson's claim that Kutuzov deliberately hung back from a direct clash with Napoleon during the retreat from Moscow. Kutuzov was not a poltroon and he knew that he could destroy Napoleon by means other than open battle. Thus Wilson is probably as mistaken to indict Kutuzov as a coward as are the Soviet historians who attempt to inflate the generalissimo into an 'heroic' figure of twentieth century proportions.

If the 'natural factors' theory needs to be revised at all, it should probably be through an increasing emphasis of the *warm* weather at various stages of the campaign: the murderous heat during the long advance to Borodino, the prolonged summer which encouraged Napoleon to linger at Moscow, and finally the untimely thawing-out of the Berezina after the Emperor had literally burnt his boats.

Despite all these changes of opinion and emphasis over the decades, the treatment of the War of 1812 by Soviet historians has remained remarkably consistent. This is because all historical writing is subject to supervision by a party committee, which ensures that the resulting book or article will conform to the ideals of Marxist-Leninism and Russia's spirit of militaristic nationalism. In the words of Marshal Koniev, military historians are 'soldiers on the ideological front'.

The first task of the Soviet historian of the Tsarist period is to sort out the 'goodies' from the 'baddies' – to establish a clear distinction between those members of the ruling class who exhibited the characteristic vices of their sort, and those few people who were so distinguished by their humanity and patriotism as to be reckoned Soviet heroes before their time. However, the final pronouncement is flavoured by a strong dose of old-fashioned nationalism, and thus the old aristocrat Kutuzov is held up to veneration while the low-born semi-foreigner Barclay remains in the limbo to which he was first consigned by the tsarist historians. Kutuzov has further appealing traits. He possessed to the full the quality of slyness which Russians admire in their public men, and he reminds them of those survivors of the eighteenth century who are depicted so vividly in their classic literature: people like the wicked old duchess in Pushkin's *Queen of Spades*, or the wigged and powdered old campaigner, Prince Bolkonsky, in *War and Peace* who so abhorred superstition and idleness.

The Soviets hold Alexander in low esteem, but they reserve their particular contempt for the Tsar's foreign advisers, who are always categorised as 'opportunists' and 'adventurers'. Thus the British military historian David Chandler presented the 1970 meeting of the International Congress of Historical Sciences in Moscow with a factual review of Wilson's diary of the 1812 campaign, and was immediately attacked by a series of Russian historians who read out prepared statements of 'objective' scholarship which bore only the slightest relevance to what Mr Chandler had actually said.

As we might expect, the ordinary Russians are invariably depicted as long-enduring and heroic folk, who exercised (or ought to have exercised) an enormous influnce on historical events. Thus Garnich asserts that 'Kutuzov intended to continue the Battle of Borodino so as to destroy Napoleon's army on the field and then go over to the strategic counter-attack. He was prevented by one thing only, and that was because Alexander I and his reactionary government failed to secure for the army the essential strategic reserve of manpower. The tsarist government did not wish to take the broad popular mass into partnership in a war of national liberation. It disliked and feared the notion of creating a large and genuine popular *opolochenie*.'[23] The Russian soldiers naturally share the traits of the people from whom they sprang. They can be robbed of victory only by the efforts of corrupt governments, wicked aristocratic officers or unscrupulous foreign adventurers.

When all the histories are forgotten, the vision of the War of 1812 which will endure longest is the one presented by Tolstoy in *War and Peace* (1862-69). At one level the tale is a love story told against a background of great events, dealing with the tribulations of a quartet of young people – the feckless Nikolai Rostov and his sister Natasha, and the all-too-human Pierre Besukhov and his philosophical officer friend, Andrei Bolkonsky. For Tolstoy, however, they represent just so many human atoms out of the millions which collectively shape the course of history.

It is the same with Napoleon, Kutuzov and the other commanders who are represented so carefully and on the whole so accurately. Tolsoy believes that war is decided by 'the molecular movement of millions of individuals', and that the names of 'great men' should be associated with great events only in the way of convenient labels. Tolstoy therefore treats events on two planes – one is the overview of the grand collective experience which is called 'history', and the other is a microscopic examination of the lives of a very few of the component individuals – people who have no claim to be masters of their own fate let alone of anybody else's.

The first military scenes relate to the campaign of 1805, when we find the Russian army fighting at a disadvantage, marooned on the Danube and in Moravia, and collectively under the spell of the dim, fat, white-uniformed Austrians. All is confusion and uncertainty in the high command, though

Tolstoy's observation is needle sharp in his tactical vignettes of the fighting at Schöngraben and Austerlitz.

In Book 9 we move on to 1812 and the hubbub of the arguing factions in the Tsar's headquarters at Vilna. This time it is the Germans who are in the ascendant – fiddly, over-intelligent people, who believe that events can be subjected to rational calculation. Like the contemporary Russians of the National Party Tolstoy classifies Barclay as a kind of honorary German, who 'thinks too much, and looks at things too closely'. The intellectual soldiers are discredited by the collapse of Phull's strategy and the continuing retreat before the *Grande Armée*, but gradually the resolve of the body of the Russian army is strengthened by the appointment of Kutuzov (who is important as a totem if not as an individual) and by the desire to win back the soil of the fatherland. Tolstoy describes the process in Book 10, and he symbolises the change which came over the nation's spirit when he talks of Andrei's responses to the news that Smolensk had fallen to the enemy desecrators.

Book 10 brings us on to the Battle of Borodino, which we see mostly through the eyes of the wandering civilian Pierre Besukhov. Pierre travels to the battlefield on 6 September, and is impressed by the sight of a party of militiamen who are toiling away at one of the batteries near Gorki. He surveys the endless fields of waving corn while a grave-faced officer explains the terrain to him, and he sees the icon of Smolensk carried before the regiment. Finally he travels to the left wing in the company of Bennigsen who moves Tuchkov's troops out of their ambush position in the woods.

The battle opens with the stupendous bombardment, of which Tolstoy gives a magnificent impression. Pierre gets caught up with a regiment which is marching towards the fight for the bridge across the Kolocha at Borodino, but he disentangles himself and makes his way past VI Corps and up to the Raevsky Redoubt shortly before Morand's attack comes in. He is sent towards an ammunition cart, which blows up in his face, and returns to the battery in time to find it in the hands of the French. He then stumbles down the ravine on the rearward side of the redoubt hill and runs into Ermolov's counter-attack. During all this time Andrei's regiment has remained in reserve, but at two in the afternoon it is moved to the sector between the Raevsky Redoubt and Semenovskaya, and Pierre's friend falls victim to a shell which hypnotises him by its spinning and finally explodes to lethal effect. Andrei's regiment probably formed part of Tolstoy's IV Corps, and the deadly shell almost certainly came from one of Sorbier's six-inch howitzers.

Tolstoy is much less convincing when he takes us to the rival headquarters during the battle. The strange inactivity of Napoleon and Kutuzov on this particular day certainly fits in well with Tolstoy's odd ideas about the powerlessness of individual human beings; even so he presents the commanders as little more than caricatures. He portrays the Emperor (of all people) as a passive tool in the hands of his army, which would have done away with him if he had tried to restrain them from fighting the Russians and reaching Moscow. Kutuzov is supposed to have been forced to give battle on ground that was none of his own choosing, though he wisely spent the day slumped down and lethargic, guiding 'the spirit of the army' by some mysterious process rather than devising futile tactical dispositions. Thus the Russians managed to quell the enemy by moral force, even though they suffered such heavy casualties in the process that they had to abandon the field.

In Books 13, 14 and 15 it is the same 'spirit of the army' which assumes control even of Kutuzov, forcing him against his will to go over to the active counter-attack. One of the human casualties of the process is Nikolai Rostov, killed in a hare-brained charge against the retreating French.

In his study of the historiography of *War and Peace* R. F. Christian has shown that Tolstoy wrote against the background of a general revival of interest in patriotic history in the 1860's. He drew most heavily on the standard works of Mikhailovsky-Danilevsky, though he also read the published eyewitness accounts of Glinka, Davydov and Rodozhitsky. The cunning device of taking the reader on an explanatory tour of Borodino in the company of Pierre Besukhov is probably derived from Stendhal's *La Chartreuse de Parme,* which has the non-combatant Fabrice wandering on to the battlefield of Waterloo. However, Prince Vyazemsky witnessed Borodino in the capacity of a real-life 'Pierre', and he may have told Tolstoy of his recollections before he published them in his memoirs in 1869.

Almost every decade, film-makers are drawn irresistibly towards *War and Peace*. Hollywood brought out a colourful version of the epic in 1951, with a convincing Natasha (Audrey Hepburn), a light-weight Andrei (Mel Ferrer), and Henry Fonda playing a solid Pierre. The advance of the French infantry against the Raevsky Redoubt was treated in impressive style, though the cavalry charged at top speed from an impossibly remote start line and the redoubt itself was sited on a miniature alp. The director was unable to withstand the temptation of regarding the military episodes as spectacular intervals in a 'love story', and he enlivened the closing minutes of the film by a stupendous re-staging of the passage of the Berezina (which looks about as wide as the Mississippi), ignoring the fact that Tolstoy does not even mention the episode, which he regarded as insignificant.

For a sense of period we must turn to Sergei Bondarchuk's production of 1962-67, to which the Russian government devoted millions of roubles and the energies of tens of thousands of troops. Bondarchuk himself played an impressive Pierre, seconded by a suitably brooding and detached Andrei and a winsome though somewhat over-balletic Natasha (Ludmilla Savelyeva). The authenticity of the uniforms was almost faultless, though it was a pity that with such resources at his disposal Bondarchuk chose to treat the military episodes as a whole, and Borodino in particular, in such an impressionistic manner. Without the support of an intelligible narrative, the effect of mere spectacle is subject to a law of rapidly diminishing returns. Perversely enough the Russian audiences preferred the bright and unhistorical American rendering to their own production.

The British produced a rival version of the epic in the shape of a twenty-three part serial screened on BBC Television in 1972-73. The director John Davis had to fill a very wide canvas without enjoying anything like the resources that were available to Hollywood and Bondarchuk. What was lacking in cash had to be supplied by imagination, an eye for significant detail and the narrative value of Jack Pulman's explicit and authentic script. The military passages could at last be given some-

171

thing of their true prominence, aided by some excellent charac-
terisations of the major figures.

There is, of course, an inherent limitation to the insight
which histories, novels and films can give into a battle or
campaign, and some of the missing elements are best supplied
by a visit to the actual site.

Whatever his reservations about the Soviet system of government, the visitor to Russia to-day is soon convinced that the
relics of the War of 1812 have passed into appreciative hands.
The approach from Moscow to Borodino lies along the road
to Smolensk and Minsk, which runs arrow-straight through
vast forests, broken here and there by open plains where the
war memorials testify to the ferocity of the fighting in 1941
and 1942. After about sixty miles a side road to the right carries
the pilgrim through the little town of Mozhaisk and on to the
heights on the fringes of the field of Borodino where stand the
monuments marking what is alleged to be Kutuzov's command-
post outside Gorki. The road continues to the valley of the
Kolocha, whence a left fork leads to the Borodino Museum.

The field is best described as a kind of Russian Gettysburg,
part national shrine and part tourist attraction, complete with
notice-boards, monuments, souvenir-stalls and vehicle parks.
The Museum is an attractive yellow-washed building in the
neo-classical style, approached by an avenue which is flanked
by guns taken from the *Grande Armée*. The entrance is
guarded by two magnificent Russian unicorn howitzers. You
pass through little rooms adorned with uniforms, pictures and
weapons, you pause to admire a splendid floor model of the
battle, and you leave by way of an exhibition devoted to the
activity of the local partisans in World War II – the Russians,
as always, are concerned to bring their military history up to
date by linking Napoleon, Hitler and the Western Imperialists
in the same series of national enemies.

As you leave the Museum you notice a constant stream of
people who are ambling up a gentle slope opposite by a path
which leads between a double row of poplars. You follow them
and find yourself on the site of the Raevsky Redoubt. The first
sense of disappointment is rapidly overtaken by admiration for
Colonel Harting or Colonel Toll or whoever it was who first
appreciated the magnificent field of fire : the ground in front

slopes evenly away for several hundred yards in a natural killing-ground, and to the right you can make out the dazzling white tower of Borodino church and the plain which once swarmed with the horsemen of Platov and Uvarov. Nothing remains of the redoubt (indeed it was fast disappearing in the 1820's), though the lower reaches of the little hill are ringed by zig-zag trenches and battered pill boxes – part of the Outer Mozhaisk Defence Line of 1941. In a way there could be no more suitable tribute to the engineers of 1812.

Returning to the road and turning to the right, we reach the Kolocha as it crosses the battlefield transversely from south-west to north-east. The winding river is narrower and shallower than the descriptions might have led one to expect, though in many places the banks of crumbling brown earth are surprisingly steep and must have offered a considerable obstacle to the tactical formations of the day. The appearance and size of the village of Borodino can have altered very little since 1812. The church is a solidly-built whitewashed construction, standing high on a bluff. One wonders why the Russians, having chosen to hold Borodino at all, did not make something more of this very defensible position.

Retracing one's tracks across the Kolocha, past the Museum, one travels south towards the centre and left of the Russian line of battle. It is difficult to reconcile the delightful meadows and the little woods of pine and birch with the grim heath-like terrain which the contemporaries describe: perhaps the land has been more intensively cultivated since then. In these pleasant suroundings you may easily overlook the site of Semenovskaya – a few grassy ledges and mounds standing just above the little valley of the Semenovka stream.

Surprisingly soon we are among the Bagration Flèches, which were restored in 1912 on a scale which surely surpasses the original versions. The southernmost of the fortifications nevertheless repays a visit, for here the embrasures and gun-platforms are clearly traced in the earth, and at the salient we find a grave adorned with fresh flowers – the resting place of General Neverovsky. Across the gorge of the flèche stand the monuments to his heroic 27th Infantry Division and to the pioneers of the army and Konovnitsyn's 3rd Infantry Division. On the site of the rearmost flèche rises a decayed monastery building, whose chapel contains the funeral carriage of Kutuzov.

Looking west across the plain and the clumps of pine trees we see the Shevardino Redoubt on the horizon. The work has been restored in the same style as the Bagration Flèches, though the line of the original ditch may be easily traced by a trough which runs in front of the ditch of 1912. Here for the first time one feels the presence of the French, in the shape of a tall monument to the *Grande Armée* standing in the middle of the redoubt, and the little mounds which mark the sites of French batteries to the north-east and south-east. The area of the fighting around Utitsa is rather less accessible, for it is shrouded in dense pine forest and severed from the rest of the field by a railway line.

Despite revolutions and the passage of time the Russians have certainly abided by the spirit of Kutuzov's command of October, 1812: 'I humbly beg you . . . to leave these fortifications inviolate. May they decay with time, but never be destroyed by the hand of man; may the husbandman, tilling his peaceful fields, never disturb them with his plough; may they be sacred monuments of courage for the Russians of later times; may our descendants on looking at them be inspired with the flame of emulation, and say admiringly: "This was the place where the pride of those beasts of prey fell before the fearless sons of our Fatherland!"' The style of Russian rhetoric has changed surprisingly little over the years.

For the most striking visual impression of the battle we must return to Moscow and visit the excellent modern Borodino Museum, which houses amongst other things a huge circular diorama which was painted in late tsarist times by F. A. Rubo. This was the golden age of realistic military painting, and the bottom edge of the canvas blends in most cunningly with the 'glowing' embers of the village of Semenovskaya, and various items of genuine military equipment which are scattered about with artful carelessness. Our standpoint is on the northern fringe of Semenovskaya just behind the 2nd Combined Grenadier Division, and the episode is the attack of Murat's cavalry and Friant's infantry some time after ten in the morning. The diorama was moved from Borodino to Moscow in the 1960's, after it had been damaged by a maniac.

At one end of Red Square the Historical Museum has a long hall devoted to weapons, paintings and documents relating to the War of 1812. The most complete collection of Russian military portraiture of the period is however to be found in the Military Gallery of the Hermitage Palace in Leningrad, where we see a full-length painting of Tsar Alexander seated somewhat uncertainly on a prancing horse, and flanked on either side of the hall by George Dawe's portraits of dozens of his generals.

As for the Black Virgin of Smolensk, she rests in the Monastery of Zagorsk, north-east of Moscow, calmly waiting for the time when the Russians will call on her again.

NOTES

INTRODUCTION

1. Kutuzov to Alexander, 10 Sept 1812, *Borodino Dokumenty, Pis'ma, Vospominaniya*, Moscow, 1962, 117
2. Report of 14 Sept 1812, *Correspondance Diplomatique de Joseph de Maistre 1811-17*, Paris, 1860, I, 177
3. Ibid
4. Col. A. A. Strokov, *Istoriya Voennogo Iskusstva*, Moscow, 1965, 199

CHAPTER 1 THE ROOTS OF THE WAR OF 1812

1. Martin Philippson 'La Paix d'Amiens', *Revue Historique*, LXXV, Paris, 1901, 72

CHAPTER 3 NAPOLEON'S ARMY

1. Ségur, *Histoire de Napoleon*, Paris, 1825, I, 123
2. Ibid, I, 338
3. Ibid, I, 417
4. Ibid, I, 127
5. Roth von Schreckenstein, *Die Kavallerie in der Schlacht an der Moskwa*, Münster, 1858, 122

CHAPTER 4 THE RUSSIAN ARMY

1. H. Bunbury *Narratives of some Passages in the Great War with France*, ed. J. W. Fortescue, London, 1927, 26
2. Ambassador Vorontsov to Lord Grenville, 1 July, 1799, Hist Manuscripts Commission *Dropmore Papers*, London, 1892-1927, V,110
3. F. von Schubert *Unter dem Doppeladler*, Stuttgart, 1962, 94
4. Löwenstern's account, *Borodino Dokumenty*, 369
5. R. Wilson *Brief Remarks on the Character and Composition of the Russian Army*, London, 1810, 1
6. Alexander to Barclay, summing up the reforms, 12 Oct 1810, Russian Gen Staff *La Guerre Nationale de 1812*, Fr trans 1902-c14, I, pt2, 32
7. Barclay to Lieutenant-General Steinheil, 9 June 1810, ibid, I, pt1, 94
8. Ibid, I, pt1, 144
9. Russian Gen Staff *Stoletie Voennago Ministerstva*, St Peters-

burg 1902-13, IV, pt1, bkII, section 3, *Ustavy i Nastavleniya*, 225
10. Ibid, 230
11. *Brief Remarks*, 13
12. Ibid, 19
13. Ibid, 38
14. Dumonceau *Mémoires*, Brussels, 1960, 121
15. *Brief Remarks*, 20
16. *Ustavy i Nastavleniya*, 316
17. *Schubert*, 69
18. Ibid, 22
19. *Brief Remarks*, 47
20. Wolzogen *Memoiren*, Leipzig, 1851, 46
21. Schubert, 194

CHAPTER 5 THE INVASION

1. Löwenstern in *Napoleons Untergang*, Stuttgart, undated, 101
2. Schubert, 216
3. Wolzogen, 120
4. Schubert, 219
5. Löwenstern in *Napoleons Untergang*, 105
6. Ségur, I, pt1, 264
7. Dumonceau, 118
8. Ibid, 118

CHAPTER 6 KUTUZOV TAKES COMMAND

1. F. Glinka *Ocherki Borodinskago Srazheniya*, Moscow, 1839, 5
2. L. N. Punin *Fel'dmarshal Kutuzov*, Moscow, 1957, 21
3. Strokov, 153
4. Wolzogen, 132
5. R. Wilson *Narrative of Events during the Invasion of Russia*, London, 1860, 131
6. Wolzogen, 40
7. A. N. Murav'ev in *Borodino Dokumenty*, 373
8. A. B. Golitsyn in *Borodino Dokumenty*, 343
9. Letter of 1 Sept, in *Borodino Dokumenty*, 42
10. To Chichagov, 1 Sept, in *Borodino Dokumenty*, 46
11. *Borodino Dokumenty*, 26
12. Murav'ev in *Borodino Dokumenty*, 373
13. I. I. Rodozhitsky in *Borodino Dokumentry*, 383
14. Davydov, *Voennye Zapiski*, Moscow, 1940-49, 198-99
15. Ibid, 206

CHAPTER 7 MAKING READY FOR THE BATTLE

1. Anonymous account of the battle, *Borodino Dokumenty*, 318
2. Undated report, late Sept, *Borodino Dokumenty*, 135
3. As spoken to Ensign Shcherbinin, *Borodino Dokumenty*, 395
4. A. A. Shcherbinin, in *Borodino Dokumenty*, 396
5. *Borodino Dokumenty*, 397
6. *Kutuzov Sbornik*, IV, pt1, 129
7. In P. Holzhausen *Die Deutschen in Russland*, Berlin, 1912, I, 82-83
8. *Borodino Dokumenty*, 383
9. *Borodino Dokumenty*, 351
10. *General Bagration. Sbornik Dokumentov*, Moscow, 1945, 241
11. *Borodino Dokumenty*, 377
12. Wolzogen, 138
13. E. Labaume, *Circumstantial Narrative*, London, 1815, 127
14. Griois, *Mémoires*, Paris, 1909, II, 29
15. Gorgaud, *Napoléon et la Grande Armée*, Paris, 1825, 205
16. *Borodino Dokumenty*, 345
17. Labaume, 130
18. *Borodino Dokumenty*, 350
19. *Borodino Dokumenty*, 331
20. *Borodino Dokumenty*, 331
21. Ségur, I, 377
22. Ibid, I, 377
23. Ibid, I, 378
24. Rodozhitsky, in *Borodino Dokumenty*, 385
25. Mikhailovsky-Danilevsky, *Opisanie Otechestvennoi Voiny*, St Petersburg 1839-40, II, 228
26. Murav'ev, in *Borodino Dokumenty*, 376
27. Strokov, 183
28. *Borodino Dokumenty*, 89-90
29. *Kutuzov, Sbornik*, IV, pt1, 139
30. Baron von Helldorf's account, *Napoleons Untergang*, 159-60
31. Gorgaud, 212
32. Ségur, I, 379-80
33. Combe *Mémoires*, Paris, 1896, 83
34. Holzhausen, I, 82
35. H. von Brandt, in *Napoleons Untergang*, 66
36. Ségur, I, 386
37. Rapp, *Mémoirs*, Paris, 1823, 201
38. Ségur, I, 388
39. Dumonceau, 136
40. Rodozhitsky in *Borodino Dokumenty*, 385

41. Bogdanov in *Borodino Dokumenty*, 338
42. *Borodino Dokumenty*, 328
43. *Borodino Dokumenty*, 338

CHAPTER 8 THE BATTLE OF 7 SEPTEMBER

I. The opening bombardment. The first attacks of the Grande Armée

1. Rodozhitsky in *Borodino Dokumenty*, 386
2. *Borodino Dokumenty*, 386
3. *Borodino Dokumenty*, 391
4. Roth von Schreckenstein, 47
5. Wolzogen, 143
6. Kutuzov to Alexander, undated, late Sept, *Borodino Dokumenty*, 136
7. *Borodino Dokumenty*, 361
8. Löwenstern in *Borodino Dokumenty*, 363
9. Löwenstern in *Borodino Dokumenty*, 362
10. Ségur, I, 390
11. Dumonceau, 135-36
12. Löwenstern to Kutuzov, *Borodino Dokumenty*, 184
13. *Borodino Dokumenty*, 353
14. Kutuzov to Alexander, Sept, *Borodino Dokumenty*, 137
15. Helldorf's account in *Napoleons Untergang*, 164
16. Ibid, 166

II. The Battle for the Bagration Flèches

1. Girod de l'Ain *Souvenirs*, Paris, 1873, 258
2. *Borodino Dokumenty*, 342
3. Col. Stockmayer's account, Holzhausen, 91
4. Strokov, 200
5. Ibid, 190
6. Ibid, 201
7. Murav'ev in *Borodino Dokumenty*, 377
8. Löwenstern in *Borodino Dokumenty*, 365

III. The first attacks on the Raevsky Redoubt

1. General Kreutz in *Borodino Dokumenty*, 359
2. *Borodino Dokumenty*, 381
3. G. Bertin, *La Campagne de 1812*, Paris, undated, 92
4. Ermolov to Barclay, 2 Oct, *Borodino Dokumenty*, 171
5. Wolzogen, 141
6. Davydov, 198
7. *Borodino Dokumenty*, 333
8. Glinka, 68

179

9. Ermolov in *Borodino Dokumenty*, 355
10. Helldorf in *Napoleons Untergang*, 167-68
11. *Borodino Dokumenty*, 334

IV. The fall of Semenovskaya and the crisis of the Russian centre

1. Shcherbinin in *Borodino Dokumenty*, 398
2. Holzhausen, I, 93
3. Ibid, I, 95
4. *Borodino Dokumenty*, 358
5. Mikhailovsky-Danilevsky, II, 252
6. Colonel Kutuzov, in ibid, II, 251
7. Ségur, I, 396
8. Boulart *Mémoires*, Paris, undated, 254-55
9. Ségar, I, 402
10. Lejeune, in Bertin, 74
11. Ségur, I, 399
12. This point is emphasised in Gorgaud, 225

V. Uvarov's diversion

1. To Löwenstern, *Borodino Dokumenty*, 367
2. Combe, 88
3. *Borodino Dokumenty*, 383
4. Golitsyn in *Borodino Dokumenty*, 343
5. *Borodino Dokumenty*, 356
6. *Borodino Dokumenty*, 377
7. The 6th, 8th and 25th Chasseurs à Cheval, La Haussaye's dragoon division and two regiments of Italian dragoons, as well as General Ornano's eight regiments (9th and 19th Chasseurs à Cheval, the 2nd and 3rd Italian Chasseurs à Cheval, and the 3rd, 4th, 5th and 6th Bavarian Chevauxlegers).
8. *Borodino Dokumenty*, 354
9. *Borodino Dokumenty*, 363
10. Schubert, 234

VI. The fall of the Raevsky Redoubt

1. Roth von Schreckenstein, 47-48
2. Griois, 36
3. Lejeune, in Bertin, 73
4. *Borodino Dokumenty*, 334
5. Roth von Schreckenstein, 93
6. Labaume, 142
7. Rodozhitsky in *Borodino Dokumenty*, 388
8. Von Meerheim's account in Holzhausen, 101

9. Ibid, 101
10. Labaume, 143
11. *Napoleons Untergang*, 67
12. Roth von Schreckenstein, 121
13. Ibid, 109
14. Barclay in *Borodino Dokumenty*, 335
15. Strokov, 195
16. *Borodino Dokumenty*, 390

VII. The final stages of the battle
1. Clausewitz *Der Feldzug von 1812*, 1862, 136-37
2. Lejeune, in Bertin, 76
3. Wolzogen, 145-46
4. *Borodino Dokumenty*, 95-96
5. Wolzogen, 147
6. Kutuzov to Alexander, Sept, *Borodino Dokumenty*, 141
7 Bernhardi, *Toll*, Leigzig, 1865, II, 114
8. Kutuzov to Alexander, Sept, *Borodino Dokumentv*, 144
9. *Borodino Dokumenty*, 344
10. P. A. Zhilin, *Gibel' Napoleonovskoi Army*, Moscow, 1968, 136
11. *Borodino Dokumenty*, 378
12. Wolzogen, 148
13. Labaume, 151
14. Ségur, I, 418
15. Bertin, 93
16. Roth von Schreckenstein, 21
17. Caulaincourt, *Memoirs*, London, 1950, I, 247-48
18. Roth von Schreckenstein, 4

CHAPTER 9 THE RECKONING
1. Roth von Schreckenstein, 134
2. 'Borodinskoe Srazhenie', in *Polkovodets Kutuzov*, Moscow, 1955, 244
3. Zhilin, 136
4. Ibid
5. *Campaigns of Napoleon*, London, 1966, 807
6. *Borodino Dokumenty*, 398
7. Roth von Schreckenstein, 5
8. *Borodino Dokumenty*, 343
9. *Borodino Dokumenty*, 342
10. *Borodino Dokumenty*, 188

1. *Kutuzov, Sbornik*, IV, pt1, 221
2. Holzhausen, 120
3. Clausewitz, 155
4. *Kutuzov, Sbornik*, IV, pt1, 277
5. Ibid, IV, pt2, 33-34
6. Ibid, IV, pt2, 292
7. Davydov, 268
8. *Kutuzov, Sbornik*, IV, pt1, 301
9. Ibid, IV, pt2, 147-48
10. Bernhardi, II, 231
11. Holzhausen, 139
12. C. de Grunwald, *La Campagne de Russie*, Paris, 1863, 248
13. Strokov, 217
14. Holzhausen, 12
15. Labaume, 271-72
16. *Kutuzov, Sbornik*, IV, pt2, 110
17. Strokov, 217
18. *Kutuzov, Sbornik*, IV, pt2, 139
19. Labaume, 287
20. *Kutuzov, Sbornik*, IV, pt2, 239
21. Ibid, IV, pt2, 198
22. *General Wilson's Journal*, London, 1964, 260
23. Marbot, *Mémoires*, Paris, 1891, III, 206-07
24. *Kutuzov, Sbornik*, IV, pt2, 423
25. Labaume, 390-91
26. Zhilin, 266, 68,000 of the flanking forces retreated un-
    scathed. Conversely more than 100,000 of the supporting
    troops were lost when the Polish and East German for-
    tresses fell during the following year.

CHAPTER 11 BORODINO IN HISTORY AND FICTION

1. *Opisanie Voiny 1812 Goda*, St Petersburg
2. *Istoriya Nashestviya Imperatora Napoleona*, St Petersburg,
   eds of 1824 and 1837
3. *Opisanie Otechestvennoi Voiny v 1812 Godu*, St Petersburg,
   1839-40
4. Mikhailovsky-Danilevsky, I, xv
5. *Istoriya Otechestvennoi Voiny 1812 Goda*, St Petersburg,
   1859-60
6. *Otechestvennaya Voina 1812 Goda*, 1900-17
7. A. V. Gerua, *Borodino*, St Petersburg, 1912, and B. M. Kolyubakin, *1812 God Borodinskoe Srazhenie*, St Petersburg,
   1912

8. *Otechestvennaya Voina 1812 i Russkoe Obshchestvo*, ed A. K. Dzhivelegov, 1911-12
9. *Nashestvie Napoleona*, Moscow, 1941
10. F. R. Klokman, 'Voprosy Voennoi Istory Rossy XVIII—Nachala XIX v. v Sovetskoi Istoriografy', in *Voprosi Voennoi Istory Rossy XVIII i Pervaya Polovina XIX Vekov*, ed L. G. Beskrovny, Moscow, 1969, 25
11. In the collection *Dvadtsat' Pyat' Let Istoricheskoi Nauki v SSSR*, 1942
12. 'Suvorov kak Predstavitel' Russkogo Voennogo Iskusstva', in *Istorichesky Zhurnal*, XII, 1941
13. *Kutuzov, Sbornik* and *General Bagration, Sbornik*
14. Klokman, 28
15. Garnich, 235
16. *Narodnoe Opolchenie v Otechestvennoi Voine 1812 Goda*, ed L. G. Beskrovny, Moscow, 1962
17. *Otechestvennaya Voina 1812 Goda*, Moscow, 1962
18. Moscow, 1962
19. *Gibel' Napoleonovksoi Army v Rossy*, Moscow, 1968
20. Ibid, 4
21. *Nashestvie Napoleona*
22. *Russkaya Istoriya v samon szhatom Ocherke*, Moscow, 1967
23. Garnich, 246-47

BIBLIOGRAPHY

D. I. Akhsharumov *Opisanie Voiny 1812 Goda*, St Petersburg, 1819. *General Bagration. Sbornik Dokumentov i Materialov*, ed S. N. Golubov and F. E. Kuznetsov, Moscow, 1945.
Mémoires du Général Bennigsen, 3 Vols, Paris, c. 1906.
T. von Bernhardi *Denkwürdigkeiten aus dem Leben des Kaiserl. Russ. Generals von der Infanterie Carl Friedrich Grafen von Toll*, 4 pts, Leipzig, 1865. One of the sources used by Tolstoy. Indispensable for the construction of a detailed narrative of the battle.
G. Bertin *La Campagne de 1812 d'après des Témoins Oculaires*, Paris, undated. With the accounts of Baron Lejeune, Count Roman Soltyk and Captain François.
Ed. L. G. Beskrovny *Voprosi Voennoi Istory Rossy XVIII i Pervaya Polovina XIX Vekov*, Moscow, 1969. Contains V. A. D'yakov 'Ob Osobennostyakh Razvitiya Russkoi Voenno-Istoricheskoi Mysli v Predreformennoe Tridtsatiletie', on the treatment of the War of 1812 by tsarist historians. Also Iu. R. Klokman 'Voprosy Voennoi Istory Rossy XVIII – Nachala XIX V. v Sovetskoi Istoriografy', a bibliography of Soviet military histories of the early 1800's.
M. I. Bogdanovich *Istoriya Otechestvennoi Voiny 1812 Goda po Dostovernym Istochnikam*, 3 vols, St Petersburg, 1859-60.
Borodino Dokumenty, Pis'ma, Vospominaniya, ed. R. E. Alt'-shuller and G. V. Bogdanov, Moscow, 1962. An invaluable collection of official correspondence and eyewitness reports.
Mémoires Militaires du Général Boulart, Paris, undated. He was a major in the artillery of the Imperial Guard.
A. Brett-James *Eyewitness Accounts of Napoleon's Defeat in Russia*, London, 1966.
D. P. Buturlin *Istoriya Nashestviya Imperatora Napoleona na Rossiyu v 1812-m Godu*, St Petersburg, eds of 1824 and 1937.
Memoirs of General de Caulaincourt, Duke of Vicenza, 3 vols, London, 1850. He was Master of Horse in Napoleon's household, and brother of the General Caulaincourt killed at the Raevsky Redoubt.
D. G. Chandler *The Campaigns of Napoleon*, London, 1967. An indispensable source book.
R. F. Christian *Tolstoy's 'War and Peace'. A Study*, Oxford, 1962.

184

C. von Clausewitz' Der Feldzug von 1812 in Russland; vol. VII of *Hinterlassene Werke*, Berlin, 1862.

Les Cahiers du Capitaine Coignet (1799-1815), Paris, 1894.

Mémoires du Colonel Combe, Paris, 1896. An officer in the 8th Chasseurs.

D. Davydov *Voennye Zapiski*, Moscow, 1940.

General Dragomiroff *Guerre et Paix de Tolstoi au Point de Vue Militaire*, Paris, 1896.

Mémoires du Géneral François Dumonceau, 1812-1813, ed J. Puraye, Brussels, 1960.

Duc de Fezensac *Souvenirs Militaires*, Paris, 1863.

N. F. Garnich 'Borodinskoe Srazhenie' in Polkovodets Kutuzov, ed. L. G. Beskrovny, Moscow, 1955. Greatly exaggerates Kutuzov's rôle in the battle. Some of the detail of the action around the Bagration Flèches is rather suspect.

A. V. Gerua *Borodina*, St Petersburg, 1912.

Russian General Staff *Otechestvennaya Voina 1812 Goda*, 24 vols. St Petersburg 1900-17. Trans by French General Staff *La Guerre Nationale de 1812*. Especially on the pre-war reforms.

Russian General Staff *Stoletie Voennago Ministerstva*, St Petersburg 1902-13. Commemorates the centenary of the War Ministry. Much material on all aspects of Russian military history, esp the codes and regulations in force in the 1800's in vol IV.

General Girod de l'Ain *Dix Ans de mes Souvenirs Militaires*, Paris, 1873. He was an officer in Desaix's division.

F. Glinka *Ocherki Borodinskago Srazheniya, Moscow*, 1839. Glorifies Kutuzov.

General Gorgaud *Napoléon et la Grande Armée en Russie, ou Examen Critique de l'Ouvrage de M. le Comte Ph. de Ségur*, Paris, 1825. By one of Napoleon's aides-de-camp. A needful corrective to Ségur's well-known account.

Mémoires Militaires du Géneral Griois 1792-1822, 2 vols. Paris, 1909. Commanded the artillery of Montbrun's cavalry corps.

C. de Grunwald *La Campagne de Russie*, Paris 1963. A collection of abbreviated and paraphrased eyewitness accounts. For this reason to be used with some caution.

B. Hollingsworth, 'The Napoleonic Invasion of Russia and Recent Soviet Historical Writing', in *The Journal of Modern History*, XXXVIII, no. 1, London, 1966.

R. Holmes, *Borodino*, London, 1971. The most convenient and up-to-date survey of the battle.

P. Holzhausen, *Die Deutschen in Russland*, 2 vols. Berlin, 1912. Eyewitness accounts from the German contingents in Napoleon's army.

Borodinskoe Srazhenie. Izdanie Imperatorskago Obshchestva Istory i Drevnostei Rossyskikh pri Moskovskom Universitete, Moscow, 1872. A detailed bibliographical study, chiefly of Bogdanovich and Mikhailovsky-Danilevsky.

M. Jenkins, *Arakheev, Grand Vizier of the Russian Empire*, London, 1969. A partial vindication of the famous old monster.

F. M. Kircheisen, *Napoleons Untergang . . . Ausgewählte Memoirenstücke*, Stuttgart, undated. For the accounts of Brandt, Löwenstern and Helldorf.

B. M. Kolyubakin, *1812 God. Borodinskoe Srazhenie 26 Avgusta*, St Petersburg, 1912.

Kutuzov M.I. Sbornik Dokumentov, ed L. G. Beskrovny, 4 vols. Moscow, 1950-56.

E. Labaume, *A Circumstantial Narrative of the Campaign in Russia*, Eng trans, 3rd ed, London, 1815. For events on the French left at Borodino.

Mémoires du Général Marbot, 91st ed, 3 vols, Paris, 1891. Lt-*1812 Godu*, 4 vols. St Petersburg 1839-40.

Gen. Mikhailovsky-Danilevsky, *Opisanie Otechestvennoi Voiny v* M. V. Nechkina and others, *1812 God*, Moscow, 1962.

Maj.-Gen. N. Okouneff, *Considérations sur les Grandes Opérations de la Campagne de 1812*, Brussels 1841.

D. Olivier, *The Burning of Moscow 1812*, London 1966. The author lays the responsibility on Rostopchin.

A. Palmer, *Napoleon in Russia*, London 1967. An excellent account from a wide variety of sources.

L. N. Punin, *Fel'dmarshalKutuzov*, Moscow 1957. Hagiography relieved by some interesting asides.

Mémoires du Généal Rapp, Paris 1823.

H. Roos, *Souvenirs d'un Médecin de la Grande Armée*, Paris 1913. Surgeon to the 3rd Württemburg Chasseurs à Cheval.

Roth von Schreckenstein, *Die Kavallerie in der Schlacht an der Moskwa . . . 1812*, Münster 1858. By a Saxon officer in Latour-Maubourg's corps. The product of personal experience and careful research, and probably the most useful account written by a survivor of the battle.

F. von Schubert *Unter dem Doppeladler. Erinnerungen eines deutschen in russischem Offiziersdienst 1789-1814*, Stuttgart 1962. By one of Barclay's staff officers. Many illuminating asides on the Russian army and its campaigns.

General Comte de Ségur *Histoire de Napoléon et de la Grande Armée pendant l'Année 1812*, 3rd ed, Paris 1825. Vivid. Far from reliable on matters of detail.
186

Mémoires Militaires du Baron Seruzier, Paris c. 1894. A colonel of light infantry. Took part in the attacks against the Bagration Flèches.

F. von Stein *Geschichte des russischen Heeres vom Ursprunge desselben bis zur Thronbesteigung des Kaisers Nikolai I Pawlowitsch*, Hanover 1885. Esp. for organisations and uniforms.

Col. A. A. Strokov *Istoriya Voennogo Iskusstva*, Moscow 1965. A good narrative. Also useful on the Russian military background.

K. von Suckow *Aus meinem Soldatenleben*, Stuttgart 1862. An officer in one of Napoleon's German contingents.

E. V. Tarle and others *Nashestvie Napoleona na Rossiyu 1812 Goda*, Moscow 1941.

Sir Robert Wilson: —
— *Brief Remarks on the Character and Composition of the Russian Army*, London 1810.
— *General Wilson's Journal 1812-1814*, ed A. Brett-James, London 1964.
— *Narrative of Events during the Invasion of Russia*, London 1860
— *A Sketch of the Military and Political Power of Russia, in the Year 1817*, 3rd ed, London 1817.

Memoiren des königlich Preussischen Generals der Infanterie Ludwig Freiherrn von Wolzogen, Leipzig 1851. Barclay's *éminence grise*. A well-informed but detached view of the campaign.

Gen. P. A. Zhilin *Gibel' Napoleonovskoi Army s Rossy*, Moscow 1968.

APPENDIX

THE ORDERS OF BATTLE AT BORODINO

A. THE GRANDE ARMEE

HEADQUARTERS AND STAFF
Chief of Staff: Marshal Berthier.
Cavalry commander: Joachim Murat, King of Naples
Artillery commander: General Laribossière.
Engineer commander: General Chasseloup.

Staff personnel
About twenty generals and four hundred officers.
Staff escort

Gensdarmes d'EliteR. (regiment)		2 sqs.
7th C.-à-C. (Chasseur à Cheval)R.		4 sqs.

IMPERIAL GUARD
Old Guard Marshal Lefebvre, Duke of Danzig.

1st Div. Gen. Delaborde

Brig. Berthezène	4th Gd.Tir. (tirailleur)R.	2 bns.
	4th Gd.Vol. (voltigeur)R.	2 bns.
	5th Gd.Vol.R.	2 bns.
Brig. Lanusse	5th Gd.Tir.R.	2 bns.
	6th Gd.Tir.R.	2 bns.
	6th Gd.Vol.R.	2 bns.

3rd Div. Gen. Curial

Brig. Boyer	1st Ch. (Chasseur)R.	2 bns.
	2nd Ch.R.	2 bns.
	1st Gr. (Grenadier)R.	2 bns.
	2nd Gr.R.	2 bns.
	3rd Gr.R.	2 bns.

Young Guard Marshal Mortier, Duke of Treviso.

Div. Gen. Roguet

Brig. Lanabèze	1st Gd. Vol.R.	2 bns.
	1st Gd. Tir.R.	2 bns.

Brig. Boyledieu	Gd. Fusilier Ch.R.	2 bns.
	Gd. Fusilier Gr.R.	2 bns.
	Gd. Flanquer Gr.R.	1 bn.
	Gd. Flanquer Gr.R.	1 bn.

Legion of the Vistula (Pol.) Gen. Claparède.

Brig. Chlopicki	1st Vistula LegionR.	3 bns.
	2nd ,, ,,	3 bns.
Brig. Bronikowski	3rd ,, ,,	3 bns.
	4th ,, ,,	3 bns.

Guard Cavalry Marshal Bessières.

1st Brigade	Brig. St. Sulpice	Gd. Dr. (Dragoon)R.	4 sqs.
		Gd. Gr.-à-C.R.	4 sqs.
2nd Brigade	Brig. Guyot	Gd. C.-à-C.R.	4 sqs.
		Mamelukes	1 sq.
3rd Brigade	Brig. Colbert	1st Gd.L. (Lancer)R. (Pol)	4 sqs.
		2nd Gd.L.R. (Dutch)	4 sqs.

Other attached troops

Portuguese C.-à-C.R.	3 sqs.
7th Chevauxlegers R. (Fr. and Pol.)	4 sqs.
Velites of Prince Borghese (It.)	1 bn.
Velites of the Tuscan Gd. (It.)	1 bn.

Guard Artillery Gen. Sorbier.

I CORPS. MARSHAL DAVOUT, PRINCE OF ECKMUHL

1st Div. Gen. Morand (attached to IV Corps)

Brig. D'Alton	13th L.I. (Light Infantry)R.	5 bns.
Brig. Gratien	17th L.I.R.	5 bns.
Brig. Bonamy	30th I.R. (Inf. Regiment)	5 bns.

2nd Div. Gen. Friant

Brig. Dufour	15th L.I.R.	5 bns.
Brig. Vandedem	33rd I.R.	5 bns.
Brig. Grandeau	48th I.R.	5 bns.
	Joseph Napoleon I.R. (Sp.)	2 bns.

3rd Div. Gen. Gérard

Gen. Gerard	7th L.I.R.	5 bns.
Brig. Desailly	12th I.R.	5 bns.
Brig. Leclerc	21st I.R.	5 bns.
	127th I.R. (Mecklenburg)	2 bns.
	8th R. of Rhine Confederation	1 bn.

4th Div. Gen. Desaix

Brig. Barbanegre	33rd L.I.R.	4 bns.
Brig. Fréderichs	85th I.R.	5 bns.
Brig. Leguay	108th I.R.	5 bns

5th Div. Gen. Compans

Brig. Duppelin	25th I.R.	5 bns.
Brig. Teste	57th I.R.	5 bns.
Brig. Guyordet	61st I.R.	5 bns.
	11th I.R.	5 bns.

Attached Cavalry Gen. Girardin

1st Lt. Brigade	Gen. Pajol	2nd C.-à-C.R.	4 sqs.
		9th L.R. (Pol.)	4 sqs.
2nd Lt. Brigade	Gen. Bourdesoul	1st C.-à-C.R.	4 sqs.
		3rd C.-à-C.R.	4 sqs.

Corps Artillery Gen. Pernety.

III CORPS. MARSHAL NEY, DUKE OF ELCHINGEN

10th Div. Gen. Ledru

Brig. Gengoult	24th L.I.R.	4 bns.
	1st Port.I.R.	2 bns.
Brig. Morion	146th I.R.	4 bns.
Brig. Bruny	72nd I.R.	4 bns.
	129th I.R. (Oldenburg)	2 bns.

11th Div. Gen. Razout

Brig. Joubert	4th I.R.	4 bns.
	18th I.R.	4 bns.
Brig. Compère	Illyrian I.R.	4 bns.
	2nd Port. I.R.	2 bns.
Brig. D'Henin	93rd I.R.	4 bns.

25th (Württ) Div. Gen. Marchand

Brig. v. Hügel	1st I.R. Prinz Paul	2 bns.
	4th I.R.	
Brig. v. Koch	2nd I.R. Herzog Wilhelm	2 bns.
	6th I.R. Kronprinz	2 bns.
Brig. v. Brüsselle	1st Jg. (Jaeger) Bn.König	
	2nd Jg. Bn.	
	1st L.I. Bn.	
	2nd L.I. Bn.	
	7th I.R.	2 bns.

190

Attached Cavalry Gen. Wollwarth

9th Li. Brigade	Gen. Mouriez	11th Hus. (Hussar)R.	4 sqs.
		6th C.-à-C.R.	4 sqs.
		4th C.-à-C.R.	4 sqs.
14th Li. Brigade	Gen. Beurmann	1st Württ Chevauxlegers R.	
		2nd Württ Chevauxlegers R.	
		3rd Württ Chevauxlegers R.	

Corps artillery Gen. Foucher

IV Corps. Prince Eugene de Beauharnais

Royal It.Gd.Div. Gen. Lecchi

	Honor Gd.R.	1 co.
	Royal Velite R.	2 bns.
	Line Velite R.	2 bns.
	Gd. Conscript R.	2 bns.

Attached Cavalry Gen. Triaire

	1st It.Gd.Dr.R.	4 sqs.
	Queen's Dr.R.	4 sqs.

13th Div. Gen. Delzon

Brig. Huard	8th L.I.R.	2 bns.
	84th I.R.	4 bns.
Brig. Roussel	1st Provisional Croat R.	2 bns.
	92nd I.R.	4 bns.
Brig. Guyon	106th I.R.	4 bns.

14th Div. Gen. Broussier

Brig. de Sivray	18th L.I.R.	2 bns.
	9th I.R.	4 bns.
Brig. Alméras	35th I.R.	4 bns.
	Joseph Napoleon I.R. (Sp.)	2 bns.
Brig. Pastol	53rd I.R.	4 bns.

Attached Cavalry Gen. Ornano

12th Li. Brigade	Gen. Ferrière	9th C.-à-C.R.	4 sqs.
		19th C.-à-C.R.	4 sqs.
13th Li. Brigade	Gen. Villata	2nd It.C.-à-C.R.	4 sqs.
		3rd It. C.-à-C.R.	4 sqs.

Bavarian cavalry detached from VI Corps

21st Li. Brigade	Gen. Seydewitz	3rd Bav.Chevxlg.R.	4 sqs.
		6th Bav.Chevxlg.R.	4 sqs.

| 22nd Li. Brigade | Gen. Preysing | 4th Bav.Chevxlg.R. | 4 sqs. |
| | | 5th Bav.Chevxlg.R. | 4 sqs. |

Corps Artillery Gen. Danthouard
V (Pol.) CORPS. PRINCE PONIATOWSKI
16th Div. Gen. Zayonczek

Brig. Mielzynski	3rd Pol.I.R.	3 bns.
	15th Pol. I.R.	3 bns.
Brig. Poszhowski	16th Pol.I.R.	3 bns.

18th Div. Gen. Kamieniecki

Brig. Grabowski	2nd Pol.I.R.	3 bns.
	8th Pol.I.R.	3 bns.
Brig. Wierzbinski	12th Pol.I.R.	3 bns.

Attached Cavalry Gen. Kaminski

18th Li. Brigade	Gen. Niemoiewski	1st Pol.C.-à-C.R.	4 sqs.
		12th Pol.L.R.	4 sqs.
19th Li. Brigade	Gen. Tyskiewicz	4th Pol.C.-à-C.R.	4 sqs.
20th Li. Brigade	Gen. Sulkowski	5th Pol.C.-à-C.R.	4 sqs.
		13th Pol.L.R.	4 sqs.

Corps Artillery Gen. Pelletier

VIII (Westphal.) CORPS. GENERAL JUNOT, DUKE OF ABRANTES

23rd Div. Gen. Tharreau

Brig. Demos	3rd Li.Bn.	
	2nd I.R.	3 bns.
	6th I.R.	2 bns.
Brig. Wickenberg	2nd Li.Bn.	
	3rd I.R.	2 bns.
	7th I.R.	3 bns.

24 Div. Gen. Ochs

	Elite C.CarabiniersR.	1 bn.
	Gr.Gd.R.	1 bn.
	1st Li.Bn.	
	5th I.R.	2 bns.

Attached Cavalry Gen. Chabert

24th Li. Brigade	Gen. v. Hammerstein		
		1st Hus.R.	4 sqs.
		2nd Hus.R.	4 sqs.
Westphal Gd.Cav.	Gen. Wolf	Gd.Chvxlg.R.	4 sqs.

I Reserve Cavalry Corps. General Nansouty

1st Li.Cav.Div. Gen. Bruyère

3rd Li. Brigade	Gen. Jacquinot	7th Hus.R.	4 sqs.
		9th C.-à-C.R.	4 sqs.
4th Li. Brigade	Gen. Piré	16th C.-à-C.R.	4 sqs.
		8th Hus.R.	4 sqs.
15th Li. Brigade	Gen. Niewiewski	6th Pol.L.R.	4 sqs.
		8th Pol.L.R.	4 sqs.
		Pruss.Hus.R.	4 sqs.

1st Cuir. (Cuirassier) Div. Gen. Saint-Germain

1st Brigade	Gen. Bessières	2nd Cuir.R.	4 sqs.
2nd Brigade	Gen. Bruno	3rd Cuir.R.	4 sqs.
3rd Brigade	Gen. Quenot	9th Cuir.R.	4 sqs.
		1st C.-à C.R.	4 sqs.

5th Cuir. Div. Gen. Valence

1st Brigade	Gen. Reynaud	6th Cuir.R.	4 sqs.
2nd Brigade	Gen. Dejean	11th Cuir.R.	4 sqs.
3rd Brigade	Gen. Delagrange	12th Cuir.R.	4 sqs.
		5th C.-à-C.R.	4 sqs.

II Reserve Cavalry Corps. General Montbrun

2nd Lit.Cav.Div. Gen. Sebastiani

7th Li. Brigade	Gen. Saint-Génies	11th C.-à-C.R.	4 sqs.
		12th C.-à-C.R.	4 sqs.
8th Li. Brigade	Gen. Baurth	5th Hus.R.	4 sqs.
		9th Hus.R.	4 sqs.
16th Li. Brigade	Gen. Suberwiecz	10th Pol.Hus.R.	4 sqs.
		3rd Württ.mtd.Jg.R.	4 sqs.
		Pruss.L.R.	4 sqs.

2nd Cuir.Div. Gen. Wathier

1st and 2nd Brigades	Brig. Caulaincourt	5th Cuir.R.	4 sqs.
		8th Cuir.R.	4 sqs.
3rd Brigade	Gen. Richter	10th Cuir.R.	4 sqs.
		2nd C.-à-C.R.	4 sqs.

4th Cuir.Div. Gen. Defrance

| 1st Brigade | Gen. Berkheim | 1st Mtd.Carab.R. | 4 sqs. |
| 2nd Brigade | Gen. L'Eritage | 2nd Mtd.Carabinier R. | 4 sqs. |

3rd Brigade	Gen. Ornano (personally detached to IV Corps)	
	1st Cuir.R.	4 sqs.
	4th C.-à-C.R.	4 sqs.

IV RESERVE CAVALRY CORPS. GENERAL LATOUR-MAUBOURG

4th Li.Cav.Div. Gen. Rozniecki

28th Li. Brigade	Gen. Dziemanowski	7th Pol.L.R.	4 sqs.
		2nd Pol.L.R.	4 sqs.
		15th Pol.L.R.	4 sqs.
		16th Pol.L.R.	4 sqs.
29th Li. Brigade	Gen. Turno	3rd Pol.L.R.	4 sqs.
		11th Pol.L.R.	4 sqs.
		17th Pol.L.R.	4 sqs.

7th Cuir.Div. Gen. Lorge

1st Brigade	Lt.-Gen. Thielemann	Garde du Corps R. (Sx)	4 sqs.
		Zastrow C.R. (Sx)	4 sqs.
		14th Pol.C.R.	4 sqs.
2nd Brigade	Gen. Lepel	1st Westphal C.R.	4 sqs.
		2nd Westphal C.R.	4 sqs.

III RESERVE CAVALRY CORPS. GENERAL GROUCHY
  (detached on left wing)

3rd Li.Cav.Div. Gen. Chastel

10th Li. Brigade	Gen. Gauthrin	6th C.-à-C.R.	4 sqs.
		8th C.-à-C.R.	4 sqs.
11th Li. Brigade	Gen. Gérard	6th Hus.R.	4 sqs.
		25th C.à-C.R.	4 sqs.
17th Li. Brigade	Gen. Domanget	1st Bav.Chvxlg.R.	4 sqs.
		2nd Bav.Chvxlg.R.	4 sqs.
		Prinz Albert Chvxlg.R.	
		(Sx)	4 sqs.

3rd Cuir.Div. Gen. Doumerc (Not on the battlefield; detached
  to Oudinot's II Corps)

6th Cuir.Div. Gen. La Haussaye

1st Brigade	Gen. Thiry	7th Dr.R.	4 sqs.
		23rd Dr.R.	4 sqs.
2nd Brigade	Gen. Seron	28th Dr.R.	4 sqs.
		30th Dr.R.	4 sqs.

COMBINED RUSSIAN ARMIES UNDER
GENERAL PRINCE KUTUZOV

Acting Chief of Staff: General Baron Bennigsen
FIRST WEST ARMY. GENERAL BARON BARCLAY DE TOLLY
(N.B. In both armies the infantry and jaeger regiments were of
  two field battalions each.)

II INFANTRY CORPS. LT.-GEN. BAGGOVUT

4th Div. Lt.-Gen. Prince Eugene of Württemburg

1st Brigade	Tobolsk I.R.	Col. Schreider
	Volhynia I.R.	Maj.-Gen. Rossi
2nd Brigade	Kremenchug I.R.	Col. Pyshnitskoi
	Minsk I.R.	Col. Krasavin
3rd Brigade	4th Jg.R.	
	34th Jg.R.	Col. Pillar

17th Div. Lt.-Gen. Alsufev

1st Brigade	Ryazan I.R.	Col. Oreus
	Belozersk I.R.	Lt.-Col. Kern
2nd Brigade	Brest I.R.	Maj. Chertov
	Willmanstrand I.R.	Col. Sokerev
3rd Brigade	30th Jg.R.	
	48th Jg.R.	

III CORPS. LT.-GEN. TUCHKOV

1st Gr.Div. Lt.-Gen. P. A. Stroganov

1st Brigade	Lifegd.Gr.R.	Maj. Demchenkov
	Arakcheev Gr.R.	Col. Knyazhnin
2nd Brigade	Pavlov Gr. R.	Col. Richter
	Ekatineroslav Gr.R.	Col. Krishtafovich
3rd Brigade	St. Petersburg Gr.R.	
	Tavrichesk Gr.R.	Col. Sulima

3rd Div. General Konovnitsyn

1st Brigade	Revel I.R.
	Muromsk I.R.
2nd Brigade	Chernigov I.R.
	Selenginsk I.R. (from 23rd Div.)
3rd Brigade	20th Jg.R.
	21st Jg.R.

| Attached Jg.Rs. | 11th Jg.R. |
| | 41st Jg.R. |

Other attached forces

Cossacks under Maj.-Gen. Karpov.

Moscow *opolchenie*
Two combined grenadier battalions
IV CORPS. LT.-GEN. OSTERMANN-TOLSTOI

11th Div.

1st Brigade	Kexholm I.R.
	Pernau I.R.
2nd Brigade	Polotsk I.R.
	Elets I.R.
3rd Brigade	1st Jg.R.
	33rd Jg.R.

23rd Div.

1st Brigade	Rylsk I.R.	
	Ekaterinburg I.R.	
2nd Brigade	18th Jg.R.	Maj.-Gen. Aleksopol

Attached forces

Kaporsk I.R.
1st Combined Gr.Bn. (from Rs. of 17th I.Div.)
2nd Combined Gr.Bn. (from Rs. of 11th and 23rd I.Divs.)
V CORPS. GRAND DUKE CONSTANTINE

Lifeguard I.Div. Lt.-Gen.Lavrov

1st Brigade	Preobrazhensky Lifegd.R.	
	Semenovsky Lifegd.R.	
2nd Brigade	Izmail Lifegd.R.	Col. Kutuzov
	Litovsk Lifegd.R.	Col. Udom
3rd Brigade	Lifegd.Jg.R.	
	Finland Lifegd.Jg.R.	

Attached forces

2nd Combined Grenadier Div.
1st Cuir.Div.
Chevalier Gd.R.

| 1st Brigade | Emperor's Lifegd.Cuir.R. | Lt.-Col. Harting |
| | Empresse's Lifegd.Cuir.R. | |

Attached forces
Lifegd.Dr.R. from 1st Cav.Div.

VI CORPS. GENERAL DOKHTUROV

7th Div. Lt.-Gen. Kaptsevich

1st Brigade	Pskov I.R.
	Moscow I.R.
2nd Brigade	Libau I.R.
	Sofia I.R.
3rd Brigade	11th Jg.R. (to 3rd Div.)
	36th Jg.R.

24 Div. Maj.-Gen. Likhachev

1st Brigade	Shirvan I.R.	Maj. Teplov
	Butyrsk I.R.	Col. Denisev
2nd Brigade	Ufimsk I.R .	Maj.-Gen. Tsybulsky
	Tomsk I.R.	Lt.-Col. Popov
3rd Brigade	19th Jg.R.	Col. Vuich
	40th Jg.R.	Col. Sazonov

I CAVALRY CORPS. LT.-GEN. UVAROV

1st Cav.Div.

1st Brigade	Lifegd.Dr.R. (to 1st Cuir.Div.)
	Lifegd.L.R.
2nd Brigade	Lifegd.Hus.R.
	Lifegd.Cossack R.
4th Brigade	Nizhin Dr.R.

Attached forces
Elisabetgrad Hus.R. from 2nd Cav.Div.

Cossacks under General Platov, Ataman of the Don Cossacks

Ilovaisk Cossacks
Grekov Cossacks
Khartonov Cossacks
Denisov Cossacks
Zhirov Cossacks
Part of Ataman Cossacks
Simferopol Mtd Tartars

II CAVALRY CORPS. MAJ.-GEN. KORFF

6th Cav.Brigade	Moscow Dr.R.
	Pskov Dr.R.

8th Cav.Brigade	Iziumsk Hus.R.
	Polish L.R.
9th Cav.Brigade	Courland Dr.R.
	Orenburg Dr.R.
10th Cav.Brigade	Siberian Dr.R.
	Irkutsk Dr.R.
11th Cav.Brigade	Sumy Hus.R.
	Mariupol Hus.R.

III CAVALRY CORPS. MAJ.-GEN KREUTZ

1st Brigade	Alexandria Hus.R.
	Siberian L.R.
2nd Brigade	Smolensk Dr.R.

2ND WEST ARMY. GENERAL PRINCE BAGRATION

VII CORPS. LT.-GEN. RAEVSKY

12th Div. Maj.-Gen. Vasil'chikov

1st Brigade	Smolensk I.R.
	Narva I.R.
2nd Brigade	Aleksopol I.R.
	New Ingermanland I.R.
3rd Brigade	6th Jg.R.
	41st Jg.R. (detached to III Corps)

26th Div. Maj.-Gen. Paskevich

1st Brigade	Ladoga I.R.
	Poltava I.R.
2nd Brigade	Nizhegorod I.R.
	Orel I.R.
3rd Brigade	5th Jg.R.
	42nd Jg.R.

VIII CORPS. LT.-GEN. BOROZDIN

2nd Gr.Div.

1st Brigade	Kiev Gr.R.
	Moscow Gr.R.
2nd Brigade	Astrakhan Gr.R.
	Fanagoria Gr.R.
3rd Brigade	Siberian Gr.R.
	Little Russian Gr.R.

27th Div. Lt.-Gen.Neverovsky

1st Brigade	Odessa I.R.
	Tarnopol I.R.
2nd Brigade	Vilensk I.R.
	Simbirsk I.R.
3rd Brigade	49th Jg.R.
	50th Jg.R.

Attached forces

7th Combined Gr.Div. Maj.-Gen Vorontsov
IV CAVALRY CORPS. MAJ.-GEN. SIEVERS

4th Cav.Div.

12th Cav.Brigade	Kharkov Dr.R. (dismounted)
	Chernigov Dr.R. (dismounted)
13th Cav.Brigade	Kiev Dr.R.
	New Russian Dr.R.
14th Cav.Brigade	Akhtyrka Hus.R.
	Litovsk L.R.

2nd Cuir. Div.

2nd Cuir.Brigade	Ekaterinoslav Cuir.R.
	Military Order Cuir.R.
3rd Cuir.Brigade	Glukhov Cuir.R.
	Little Russian Cuir.R.
	Novgorod Cuir.R.

INDEX

Clausewitz, C. von (1780-1831),
Prussian Colonel in R.
service: 48, 130–131
Compans, J. D., F. General:
77–78, 98
Constantine (Konstantin
Pavlovich) (1779–1831),
Grand Duke, Inspector
General of Cavalry,
commander of V Corps: 55,
63, 75, 102

Davout, L. N. (1770–1823), Prince
of Eckmühl, Marshal,
commander of I Corps: 30,
57, 84, 85, 98, 158
Davydov, D. V. (1784–1839),
R. Hussar Colonel: 68,
149
Desaix, J. M. (1764–1825), F.
General, commander of 4th
Div.: 98, 101–103
Dokhturov, D. S. (1756–1816),
R. General, commander of
VI Corps: 75, 105, 114–116,
152, 153
Dorokhov, I. S. (1762–1815),
R. Lieutenant-General,
'partisan' leader: 149

Eblé, Count, F. Engineer
General: 159
Efremov, I. E. (1774–1843),
R. Colonel, 'partisan' leader:
149
Ermolov, A. P. (1772–1861),
R. Lieutenant-General, chief
of staff of First West Army:
55, 76, 80, 86, 96, 108–109,
111, 120, 148, 150
Eugène de Beauharnais (1781–
1824), stepson of Napoleon,
Viceroy of Italy, commander
of IV Corps: 97, 105–106,
137, 152–153, 157–158

Figner, A. S., R. staff captain and
'partisan' leader: 76, 129

Glukhov, S. A., R. artillery
colonel: 101
Golitsyn, A. B., adjutant to
Kutuzov: 134
Gorchakov, A. I. (1769–1817),
Prince, R. Lieutenant-
General: 75, 79
Griois, F. General: 123
Grouchy, E. (1766–1847),
F. General, commander of III
Reserve Cavalry Corps: 86,
121

Harting, R. Lieutenant-Colonel
and staff officer: 70

Jérôme Bonaparte (1784–1860),
younger brother of Napoleon,
King of Westphalia: 17, 31,
51, 57
Junot, A. (1771–1813), Duke of
Abrantes, F. General,
commander of VIII Corps:
62

Kaptsevich, R. Lieutenant-
General, commander of 7th
Div.: 124
Karpov, A. A. (1767–1838),
R. Major-General,
commander of *opolchenie*
and cossacks: 80, 132
Khomentovsky, R. Colonel: 134
Konovnitsyn, P. P. (1764–1822),
R. Lieutenant-General,
commander of 3rd Div.: 67,
99, 102, 105–107, 112, 114,
116, 144, 150, 152
Korff, F. K. (1774–1826),
R. Major-General,
commander of II Cavalry
Corps: 134
Kretov, R. General: 114
Kudashev, N. D. (1784–1813),
Prince, R. Colonel,
commander of Lifeguard
Horse Artillery, 'partisan'
leader: 29, 149

202

Kutaisov, A. I. (1784–1812),
R. Major-General,
commander of artillery of
First West Army: 46–47, 87,
109, 140–141
Kutuzov (Golenishchev-Kutuzov),
M. I. (1745–1813), Prince,
R. Field-Marshal,
commander of the R. armies:
character, 63–65, 91, 132, 155,
170; appointed to supreme
command, 65–67; falls back
to Borodino, 66–68; prepares
for battle, 70–86, 92; at
Borodino, 27, 99–100, 102,
108–109, 119–122, 132–135;
performance at Borodino,
141–143; abandons Moscow,
144; 'partisan' war, 148–149;
counter-attack, 149–162

Latour-Maubourg, V. N. (1768–
1830, F. General,
commander of IV Reserve
Cavalry Corps: 35, 137
Lauriston, Count, F. envoy: 145
Lavrov, N. I. (d. 1822),
R. Lieutenant-General,
commander of Lifeguard
Infantry Div.: 97
Leppich, L., balloonist: 68
Likhachev, R. Major-General,
commander of 24th Div.:
111, 124, 127–131
Lobau, F. General: 116, 153
Löwenstern, W. von, R. Major-
General: 79, 96, 104

Masséna, Prince of Essling, Duke
of Rivoli, Marshal: 16
Meerheim, Saxon Cuirassier
Lieutenant: 112–113
Mikhailovsky-Danilevsky, A. I.,
historian: 163
Miloradovich, M. A. (1771–1825),
R. General: 68, 75, 110, 135,
144, 155, 158
Montbrun, L. P., F. General,

commander of I Reserve
Cavalry Corps: 35, 123
Mortier, A. E. (1768–1835), Duke
of Treviso, marshal,
commander of the Young
Guard: 152
Murat, J. (1767–1815),
brother-in-law of Napoleon,
King of Naples, marshal,
Cavalry commander: 59, 77,
103, 115–117, 122, 131, 137,
144, 146, 150, 153, 161

Napoleon Bonaparte (1769–1821),
Emperor: character, 15–17,
31; leadership, 29–30;
strategy, 29–30; tactics, 30;
invasion of Russia, 51ff.;
arrives at field of Borodino,
69ff; attacks Shevardino
Redoubt, 77–80; prepares for
battle, 81–92; at Borodino,
115–119, 131, 136;
performance at Borodino,
139, 142–143; in Moscow,
144; on the retreat, 151–162
Neverovsky, D. P. (1771–1813),
R. Lieutenant-General,
commander of 27th Div.: 61
Ney, M. (1769–1815), Duke of
Elchingen, marshal,
commander of III Corps: 85,
88, 91, 116, 157–158, 161

Ornano, Count, 'F.' Cavalry
commander: 120
Osten-Sacken, F. V. von der
(1752–1837), R. Lieutenant-
General: 157

Paskevich, I. F. (1782–1856),
R. Major-General,
commander of 26th Div.:
106, 129
Paul I. (1754–1801), Tsar: 36
Phull, E. von, Prussian Colonel,
adviser to Tsar Alexander I:
48, 53–54

Vorontsov, M. S. (1782–1856),
R. Major-General and
commander of 7th Combined
Grenadier Div.: 102
Vuich, R. Colonel, commander
of 19th Jaeger Regiment:
97, 106

Wilson, Sir R., British General:
48, 64, 155, 159, 166
Wittgenstein, P. C. (1768–1842),
R. General of Cavalry: 57,
150, 157, 159–160
Wolzogen, L. A. von (1774–1845),
Prussian General on R. staff:
48, 61, 63, 66, 77, 111,
132–133
Württemburg, Duke Alexander,
R. General: 55
Württemburg, Prince Eugene,
R. Lieutenant-General,
commander of 4th Div.:
88, 110, 111, 132

Zhilin, P. A., General and
historian: 165–166

PLACES AND EVENTS
Borodino:
Sequence of battle 7 Sept.:
opening bombardment,
95–96, 97; F. attack on
Borodino village, 96–97;
first attacks on Bagration
Flèches, 98–99; battle for
Utitsa, 99–101; fall of
Bagration Flèches, 101–105;
Bagration's wound, 105;
first attacks on Raevsky
Redoubt, 105–111; attack on
Semenovskaya and R. centre,
111–119; Uvarov's diversion,
120–122; fall of Raevsky
Redoubt, 122–131; fall of
Utitsa mound, 132; close of
battle. 130–139; casualties,
138–139

Features of the ground:
Bagration Flèches, 73, 80–82,
85, 98–105, 173; Kolocha
stream, 70, 89, 97, 105,
119–120, 135, 173; Kolotskoi
Monastery, 68–69, 121, 130;
Moskva river, 70, 76;
Raevsky Redoubt, 68, 72,
84–86, 92, 96, 105–111, 119,
121, 135–137, 141, 154, 169,
172–173; Semenovka stream,
70, 84, 89, 105, 112, 173;
Semenovskaya village, 73,
85, 105, 111–119, 122, 173;
Shevardino Redoubt, (action
of 5 Sept. 77–81), 91, 115,
174; Utitsa village and
mound, 74, 85, 119, 131–132
Berezina river, retreat of
Grande Armée over, 26–28
Nov. 1812: 159–160
'Continental System': 16–17
Drissa, entrenched camp: 55,
56
Fili, council of war 13 Sept.
1812: 144
Inkovo, action 6 Aug. 1819: 60
Ivashkovo, R. army at: 67
Kaluga: 155
Krasnyi, action 15–17 Nov.
1812: 158
Lyakhovo, action 9 Nov. 1812:
157–158
Maloyaroslavets, action 24 Oct.
1812: 153, 155
Medyn, action 24 Oct. 1812: 154
Mohilev: 57
Moscow: 144–146
Mozhaisk, R. army at: 135
Niemen river: 17, 18, 162
Orsha: 57, 159
Polotsk, action 18–19 Oct. 1812:
157
Salamanca, battle: 89
Smolensk: 59–60; battle 16–17
Aug. 1812, 61–62; on
Napoleon's retreat, 157–158;
Black Virgin of, 86, 175

205

Finland Lifeguard Jaeger R.: 112, 114, (196)

Astrakhan Grenadier R.: 115, (198)

Moscow Grenadier R.: 115, (198)

Pavlov Grenadier R.: 101, (196)

Belozersk Infantry Regiment: 101, (195)

Brest Infantry Regiment: 132, (195)

Chernigov Infantry Regiment: 102, (195)

Kremenchug Infantry Regiment: 110, 132, (195)

Minsk Infantry Regiment: 100, (195)

Muromsk Infantry Regiment: 102, (195)

Odessa Infantry Regiment: 79–80, (199)

Revel Infantry Regiment: 102, (195)

Ryazan Infantry Regiment: 132, (195)

Simbirsk Infantry Regiment: 86, (199)

Tomsk Infantry Regiment: 108, (197)

Ufimsk Infantry Regiment: 108, 111, (197)

Willmanstrand Infantry Regiment: 101, 132, (195)

1st Jaeger R.: 97, (196)

11th Jaeger R.: 74, 106, (196)

18th Jaeger R.: 108, (196)

19th Jaeger R.: 108, (197)

20th Jaeger R.: 74, (195)

21st Jaeger R.: 74, (195)

40th Jaeger R.: 108, (197)

41st Jaeger R.: 74, (198)

New Russian Dragoon R.: 99, (199)

Pskov Dragoon R.: 129, (197)

Akhtyrka Hussar R.: 99, 113, (199)

Elisabetgrad Hussar R.: 120, (197)

Iziumsk Hussar R.: 129, (198)

Lithuanian (Litovsk) Lancer R.: 99, (199)

Polish Lancer R.: 129, (198)

26th Artillery Brigade: 106

11th Artillery Co.: 98

17th Artillery Co.: 100

32nd Artillery Co.: 98

DATE DUE

APR 25 '84			
GAYLORD			PRINTED IN U.S.A.